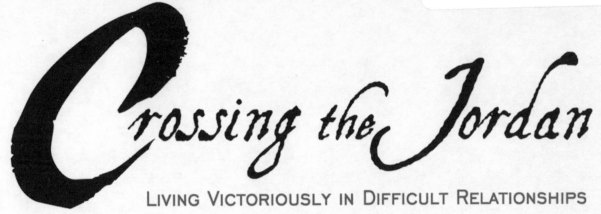

Crossing the Jordan

LIVING VICTORIOUSLY IN DIFFICULT RELATIONSHIPS

Crossing the Jordan

LIVING VICTORIOUSLY IN DIFFICULT RELATIONSHIPS

A Woman's Guide by:
Diane Hunt

America's
Keswick
*Where God speaks to hearts
and transforms lives!*

PUBLICATIONS

Fort Washington, PA 19034

Crossing the Jordan
Published by CLC Publications

U.S.A.
P.O. Box 1449, Fort Washington, PA 19034

GREAT BRITAIN
51 The Dean, Alresford, Hants SO24 9BJ

AUSTRALIA
P.O. Box 469, Kippa-Ring QLD 4021

NEW ZEALAND
118 King Street, Palmerston North 4410

ISBN-10: 1-936143-22-4
ISBN-13: 978-1-936143-22-1

Unless otherwise noted, Scripture quotations are from the Holy Bible, New King James Version, copyright © 1979, 1980, 1982 by Thomas Nelson, Inc. Used by permission. All rights reserved.

Scripture quotations marked AMP are from The Amplified Bible, © 1965 Zondervan Publishing House. Used by permission.

Scripture quotations marked ESV are from the Holy Bible, English Standard Version® copyright © 2001 by Crossway Bibles, a publishing ministry of Good News Publishers. Used by permission. All rights reserved.

Scripture quotations marked NIV are from the Holy Bible, New International Version, © 1973, 1978, 1984 by International Bible Society. Used by permission of Zondervan Bible Publishers.

Scripture quotations marked MSG are from *The Message*. Copyright © 1993, 1994, 1995, 1996, 2000, 2001, 2002. Used by permission of NavPress Publishing Group.

Italics in Scripture quotations are the emphasis of the author.

Printed in the United States of America
19 18 17 16 15 14 13 12 11   1 2 3 4 5 6

Contents

Foreword vii

Preface ix

Chapter 1   Salvation and Security 13

Chapter 2   The Sufficiency of Your Sword 23

Chapter 3   Suffering: A Tool in God's Hand 37

Chapter 4   Addiction: Idols of the Heart 45

Chapter 5   Responding Biblically in the Midst of It 59

Chapter 6   Instruments of Righteousness: Our Words, God's Purposes ... 79

Chapter 7   Anger and Bitterness 91

Chapter 8   Biblical Forgiveness 103

Chapter 9   Worry, Anxiety and Fear 119

Chapter 10   The "S Word": Submission 131

Chapter 11   The "R Word": Respect 145

Chapter 12   Intimacy with God, Our Heavenly Husband 161

Chapter 13   Marital Intimacy 173

Chapter 14   And the Journey Continues 195

Appendix: My True Identity 197

Endnotes 201

Foreword

CLC Publications has a heart for publishing "deeper-life" books with clear and timeless teachings. Keswick—a higher Christian life movement that started in 1875 in England's Lake District—has influenced many of our books, so we're excited to publish *Crossing the Jordan* with America's Keswick.

Founded in 1897, America's Keswick has spent over a hundred years delivering the message of the hope and victory found in Jesus Christ. Central to Keswick's ministry is the Colony of Mercy—a dynamic, biblical program for men struggling with addiction. As the ministry to the men developed, Keswick recognized the needs of the recovering addicts' families. As a result, the Women of Character program began, bringing the message of victorious living to the wives and fiancées of the Colony men. Reverend William Raws, Th.M., the grandson of America's Keswick's founder, described the Keswick ministry this way:

I Can't, but He Can

America's Keswick's historic message as implied in its purpose statement is that the true Christian life is not *difficult*—it's *impossible*. But the message doesn't end with that discouraging note. More than one of our conference speakers has put it this way, "the most important thing I have learned about the Christian life is that I cannot live it." They then continue with this explanation, "but God never intended me to do so." The only person who has successfully lived the Christian life is Jesus Christ. He set the standard for such a life during His days on earth as He lived as a man among men. All His life, in both attitude and action, He was totally pleasing to the Father (Matt. 3:17; John 8:29). He was totally free from sin (Heb. 4:15; 2 Cor. 5:21; 1 John 3:5). Though His conformity to the will of the godhead was tested, He was victorious.

He's in Me

Now we may be in full agreement about these facts with reference to Jesus Christ, but you may be thinking, "but I'm not Jesus." That is obvious, but it is not the whole truth. This sinless, victorious, totally pleasing person has taken up residence in the believer. If you have received Him as your Savior, He actually lives in you (Gal. 2:20). His character is to be formed in each believer by the Holy Spirit (Gal. 4:19). Listed as "the fruit of the Spirit," these virtues result from the filling of the Spirit (Eph. 5:18, Gal. 5:22–23). Jesus not only lives *in* you, but He wants to live His life *through* you. The life that He lives in you is the same kind that He lived on earth and now lives in heaven —victorious.[1]

Crossing the Jordan offers this hope of victory to women whose husbands are caught in addiction.

It's often easy to blame your problems on others and wait for them to change, but this study will challenge you to bare your heart to God, allowing yourself to be transformed by Him. Only then will you experience God's true healing power.

The authors of *Crossing the Jordan* have years of experience applying God's Word to addiction recovery counseling. With candor and insight, these counselors discuss what it's like to lean on God when it's impossible to stand on your own.

This study is interactive, so grab your pen and your Bible. (Our citations are from the New King James Version unless otherwise noted.) You'll be directed to read God's Word for yourself and answer thought-provoking questions in the blanks provided. Involve a trusted friend in this journey—you'll find it helpful to talk through the questions and experience growth together.

Just as the Israelites stood before the Jordan River thousands of years ago, you stand before your own problems today. Don't wait on the bank bemoaning your circumstances. Put your foot in the river and trust God to do the rest. We pray that as you step out in faith to face your own obstacles, you will look to God, who parts rivers and changes hearts—God, who does the impossible.

Preface

Crossing the Jordon—a compilation of writings from numerous contributors from various backgrounds and with various life-experiences—was designed for individual study as well as small group interaction. It took almost five years to complete and another three for the authors to self-publish. Now, three years later, it is being officially published so its message of freedom and victory can reach a wider audience.

We should probably define what we mean by "addiction." Addiction does not just involve alcoholism and drug abuse. In fact, we all struggle with addiction to sin because of our fallen human nature. You see, being a real support to someone who is struggling doesn't involve "fixing" the situation. Instead, your first step should be to get your own heart right with God. It's tempting, when others' sin gravely impacts you, to focus so much energy on *their* wrong choices and *their* offenses that you overlook your own. In trying to help them escape their circumstances and sin patterns, you become drained and exhausted, and you miss God's best for your own life.

Deciding what to include in this study seemed like an endless project as we added and deleted topics on a regular basis. Still, the sections are not exhaustive because our goal was for the reader to complete the study in fourteen to sixteen weeks, but we believe the contents of this book target major, key heart issues and that by applying yourself diligently to the study, together with the illumination of the Holy Spirit, you will be changed, renewed and strengthened in the midst of your circumstances. That said, unless and until you seek God's perspective, God's healing and God's truth, your hope for true freedom will never be realized. Remember that He is the only One with the power to heal all wounds.

The Jordan River was a physical barrier preventing the Israelites from entering the land God promised them that was flowing with milk and honey.

The title *Crossing the Jordan: Living Victoriously in Difficult Relationships* was chosen because it beautifully depicts the life of freedom that awaits those who choose to get their feet wet and to cross from the wilderness into the land of promise. Just like the Israelites, as you choose to step out in faith to move from your wilderness wanderings to lay hold of the promised land in your life, God will go with you. He will empower you moment by moment to lay claim to the promises of freedom and hope awaiting you on the other side of the Jordan.

> You shall write on them all the words of this law, when you have crossed over, that you may enter the land which the LORD your God is giving you, "a land flowing with milk and honey," just as the LORD God of your fathers promised you. (Deut. 27:3)

> Pass through the camp and command the people, saying, "Prepare provisions for yourselves, for within three days you will cross over this Jordan, to go in to possess the land which the LORD your God is giving you to possess." (Josh. 1:11)

> "Now therefore, take for yourselves twelve men from the tribes of Israel, one man from every tribe. And it shall come to pass, as soon as the soles of the feet of the priests who bear the ark of the LORD, the Lord of all the earth, shall rest in the waters of the Jordan, that the waters of the Jordan shall be cut off, the waters that come down from upstream, and they shall stand as a heap." So it was, when the people set

out from their camp to cross over the Jordan, with the priests bearing the ark of the covenant before the people, and as those who bore the ark came to the Jordan, and the feet of the priests who bore the ark dipped in the edge of the water (for the Jordan overflows all its banks during the whole time of harvest), that the waters which came down from upstream stood still, and rose in a heap very far away at Adam, the city that is beside Zaretan. So the waters that went down into the Sea of the Arabah, the Salt Sea, failed, and were cut off; and the people crossed over opposite Jericho. Then the priests who bore the ark of the covenant of the LORD stood firm on dry ground in the midst of the Jordan; and all Israel crossed over on dry ground, until all the people had crossed completely over the Jordan. (Josh. 3:12–17)

As the Israelites left the wilderness and crossed the Jordan into the land of promise, God's presence went with them as represented by the ark of the Lord.

Then it came to pass, when all the people had completely crossed over, that the ark of the LORD and the priests crossed over in the presence of the people. (Josh. 4:11)

Since its original publication, *Crossing the Jordan* has been an instrumental tool in impacting people's hearts and lives, aiding them in encountering the transformational power of the Holy Spirit. As you too apply the principles shared in this study, our prayer is that you will find what—or rather who—you're searching for. Jesus Christ is ready and willing to forgive and to save. Will you go to Him?

Are you ready to get your feet wet?

1

Salvation and Security

by Diane Hunt

I tell you the truth, whoever hears my word and believes Him who sent me has eternal life and will not be condemned; He has crossed over from death to life.

John 5:24

1

This chapter appears first in our study because it is foundational to everything else we will discuss. If you do not understand and receive the concepts of this chapter, the rest will simply be an academic exercise. You see, every individual can have a victorious life, but it can only be done through personal, intimate relationship with Jesus Christ. Read and study carefully, pose questions, ask God to reveal His purposes to your heart and be active in the process of seeking truth and relationship with Christ.

I may never have met you, but I know that you fit into one of two groups. Jesus said to His disciples, "If God were your Father, you would love Me, for I proceeded forth and came from God; nor have I come of Myself; but He sent Me. Why do you not understand My speech? Because you are not able to listen to My word. You are of your father the devil, and the desires of your father you want to do. He was a murderer from the beginning, and does not stand in the truth, because there is no truth in him. When he speaks a lie, he speaks from his own resources, for he is a liar and the father of it" (John 8:42–43).

There are two "families": _____ is the Father of truth. The _____ is the father of lies. Every single person belongs to one of these two families; nowhere in all of Scripture will you find a third category.

What are your thoughts on this idea? Is it new to you? _____
_____
_____
_____

"The LORD preserves all who love Him, But all the wicked He will destroy" (Ps. 145:20).

What does the Lord do for all who love Him? What does the Lord do to all the wicked? What do you think this means? _____
_____
_____

"He who believes in the Son has everlasting life; and he who does not believe the Son shall not see life, but the wrath of God abides on him" (John 3:36).

"He who is of God hears God's words; therefore you do not hear, because you are not of God" (John 8:47).

You may ask what you must do to fall into the devil's family. The answer is simple: nothing! By the nature of man, we are all born spiritually dead and separated from God. This means that we are all sinners; we all rebel against God's perfect law and will. Romans 5:12 says, "Therefore, just as through one man sin entered the world, and death through sin, and thus death spread to all men, because all sinned."

Who is the one man through whom sin entered the world? (See Genesis 3 or Romans 5:14 for help)

_____

When sin entered the world, what came with it? _____

If Adam's sin brought death, how did we end up spiritually dead? _____
_____

Read Romans 3:23. Is it just Adam's sin that condemns us? Who does it say has sinned? _____
_____
_____
_____

Do you accept the fact that you are a sinner? YES or NO

Our sin has consequences. God is a God of love, but He is also a just God and therefore must punish sin. "Yet he does not leave the guilty unpunished" (Exod. 34:7, NIV).

It is because of God's purity and holiness that He must punish sin.

Read Romans 6:23: "For the wages of sin is death, but the gift of God is eternal life in Christ Jesus our Lord."

What does this verse say we earn for sin? _____ If sin earns or deserves death and we all sin, then what do we all deserve? What is the opposite of death? _____
_____

From the moment we are conceived, we are human. We are unique. We are individuals created by God. (See Ps.139:13–16). From that moment on we are a spirit that will exist forever. Whether that life reaches birth or not, that person is an individual who will exist forever. Every person will live forever in either heaven or hell.

"And these [the unrighteous] will go away into everlasting punishment, but the righteous into eternal life" (Matt. 25:46). This verse tells us clearly that every person will receive either eternal punishment or eternal life. It also tells us who will receive eternal life. Who does it say will receive eternal life? ___
_____

If we must be righteous to have eternal life, all we have to do is live righteously, right? Look at these two verses: "There is none righteous, no, not one" (Rom. 3:10). "But we are all like an unclean thing, and all our righteousnesses are like filthy rags" (Isa. 64:6).

The outlook couldn't appear more bleak. Let's review what we have learned thus far in our study:

- ❖ Every individual person belongs to either the family of God or the family of the devil.

- ❖ We are all born spiritually dead and separated from God and therefore a member of the family of the devil.

- ❖ Every human person is a sinner.

- ❖ Sin must be punished.

- ❖ The wages of sin is death; therefore, every one of us deserves death.

- ❖ Every person ever conceived will live forever in either heaven or in hell.

- ❖ A righteous life is required to live forever in heaven.

- ❖ No human being has ever lived a perfect (righteous) life.

- ❖ By inference, there is no way any of us can save ourselves (from hell) or earn eternal life.

Well, that's the bad news. So how can we be saved?

About 2,000 years ago the disciples were asking Jesus the same question that we are asking here today: "'Who then can be saved?' But Jesus looked at them and said to them, 'With men this is impossible, but with God all things are possible'" (Matt. 19:25–26). (Note: to be "saved" is another way of saying having eternal life. One component of eternal life is living forever with God in heaven.)

Take a few minutes now to read the account of Nicodemus in John 3:1–21. We learn several things here:

Jesus told Nicodemus no one can see the kingdom of heaven unless what? (3:3) _____

What did Nicodemus think Jesus was referring to? (3:4) _____

What did Jesus mean? (3:5–6) _____

The term "born-again" has taken a lot of heat over the years. What do you think when you hear the expression "born-again"? _____

_____

For a moment set aside any preconceived notions about what it means to be born-again. Actually the phrase has a very simple explanation. Remember we learned earlier that we are all born spiritually dead and separated from God. In order for us to become spiritually alive and reconciled to God, we must be reborn in our spirit. Our spirit must be made alive or given new life so that it can go from being dead to being alive. This is it! It is that simple. A person is born-again when his spirit has been reborn or made alive. That sounds simple enough, right? Well, it is, but it is not something we can do. We do not have the means to make that happen. However, verse 6 tells us who gives birth to spirit: "That which is born of the flesh is flesh, and that which is born of the Spirit is spirit." We cannot make our spirits alive again, but the Holy Spirit of God can! Let's continue our investigation.

According to John 3:15, everyone must do what to have eternal life? _____

God tells us again a second time for emphasis in verse 16: "For God so loved the world that He gave His only begotten Son, that whoever believes in Him should not perish but have everlasting life."

What word do verses 15 and 16 have in common? _____

This word "believe" is often a stumbling block to many people. There are different meanings to this word. For instance, believe in one sense means intellectual assent. It would be the type of belief we have in historical events such as believing that Abe Lincoln was shot or that the earth was round. This is NOT the type of belief spoken of in verses 15 and 16. It is not just believing that Jesus really lived and believing the facts about His life, etc. That would be mere intellectual assent. The Scriptures say that is the type of belief that the demons have. James 2:19 says, "You believe that there is one God. You do well. Even the demons believe—and tremble!"

So now that we know what it is not, let's consider what it is to believe in such a way that it results in eternal life, as promised in verses 15 and 16. This sense of the word implies that there is a component of trust. It is not just believing that Jesus *can* save, but rather that He *does* save; He promises to save, and if you put your total trust in Him, He *will* save you. In fact, He is the only One who can save you.

Let me give an illustration to make this point. Charles Blondin, a French tightrope walker, achieved great fame for his crossings of Niagara Falls. On a small cord rigged 160 feet above the rushing water, he agilely walked across the Falls seventeen times—once blindfolded, once pushing a wheelbarrow and once stopping halfway across to prepare and eat an omelet (on a stove he carried on his back). When, in 1860, Blondin carried his assistant, Romain Mouton, across on his back, the Prince of Wales was in attendance. Now, even though the prince had heard of Blondin's success and even though he watched him confidently cross with his own eyes, when the acrobat asked the prince to hop on his back for the return journey, he quickly refused. See, he believed (intellectual assent) that Blondin could carry a man across the tightrope, but he did not believe (trust) enough to stake his life on that fact.

In the same way many people believe in Jesus. They believe all the facts about Him, but they fail to believe Him. They do not trust Him and only Him to save them.

Another great theological error is that Jesus did His part (opened the gates of heaven for us), and we must do our part (work, give money, pray and serve). I have heard it said more times than I care to count that Jesus is a crutch for those that need Him. Nothing could be further from the truth. Saying Jesus is a crutch implies that He helps the limping person into heaven. Jesus is not a crutch; He is more like a wheelchair for a complete paralytic who can do absolutely nothing to move the wheelchair. Jesus does it all. It is not Jesus and your church. It is not Jesus and your good deeds. It is not Jesus and your goodness, kindness and generosity. It is not Jesus and your service. In fact, it is not Jesus *and* anything! Through Jesus' work on the cross, He did it all.

Read John 19:28–30. What did Jesus know? (19:28) _____

What did Jesus say in verse 30? _____

_____

What was left for you to do? _____

Heaven is not something you can earn. Let's look at what God says about the salvation He provides.

Ephesians 2:8–9 tells us, "For by grace you have been saved through faith, and that not of yourselves; it is the gift of God, not of works, lest anyone should boast."

We are saved by _____

Through _____

It is a _____

Not by _____

So that no one can _____

Grace by definition is unearned, unmerited favor. You cannot earn grace. That would be an oxymoron.

Let's summarize what we have learned in this section:

✧ To be saved means to be rescued from the punishment of our sins (hell) through the saving work of Jesus Christ on the cross.

✧ Eternal life is when our spirits are made alive by the power of the Holy Spirit. We are given new life and will live forever in heaven with God. To be born-again simply means to be reborn in the spirit through the power of the Holy Spirit.

✧ To believe in Jesus unto salvation means that we trust in Christ and Him alone to save us from our sins.

✧ It is impossible for anyone to save himself. It is by grace that we are saved, through faith.

✧ Heaven is a free gift, undeserved, unearned, unmerited.

Of what we have studied thus far, what, if anything, is new to you? _____
_____
_____

Of what we have studied thus far, what is most difficult for you to accept or believe? Why? _____
_____
_____

Record any questions you may have: _____
_____
_____
_____

If we had time, we could study all the prophesies that were fulfilled by Jesus. Many things were accomplished in the thirty-three years that Jesus walked on the earth and in the final week of His earthly life. Let's focus on two aspects of the cross that are relevant to our study. The first is death; the second is life. Jesus lived the perfect life; He was without sin. Hebrews 4:15 says, "For we do not have a High Priest who cannot sympathize with our weaknesses, but was in all points tempted as we are, yet without sin." When God's wrath was poured out on Him (at the cross) it was not for His own sin, but for ours. "Surely He has borne our griefs and carried our sorrows; yet we esteemed Him stricken, smitten by God, and afflicted. But He was wounded for our transgressions, He was bruised for our iniquities; the chastisement for our peace was upon Him, and by His stripes we are healed. All we like sheep have gone astray; we have turned, every one, to his own way; and the LORD has laid on Him the iniquity of us all. . . .Yet it pleased the LORD to bruise Him; He has put Him to grief. When You make His soul an offering for sin, He shall see His seed, He shall prolong His days, and the pleasure of the LORD shall prosper in His hand" (Isaiah 53:4–6, 10).

When people think about the cross, most commonly they think about Jesus' death and the payment for sins. This is a vital component of the cross. As we learned earlier, sin brings a penalty (death). That penalty must be satisfied. We are unable to satisfy God's wrath resulting from our sin. However, God made provision through His Son Jesus Christ.

Consider Romans 8:2–4: "For the law of the Spirit of life in Christ Jesus has made me free from the law of sin and death. For what the law could not do in that it was weak through the flesh, God did by sending His own Son in the likeness of sinful flesh, on account of sin: He condemned sin in the flesh, that the righteous requirement of the law might be fulfilled in us who do not walk according to the flesh but according to the Spirit."

Jesus did what we could not do. His death on the cross was the ultimate sacrifice on our behalf. That is the first half of the cross—death, death to sin. The second half of the cross—life—is just as important. It is two sides of the same coin. "Or do you not know that as many of us as were baptized into Christ Jesus were baptized into His death? Therefore we were buried with Him through baptism into death, that just as Christ was raised from the dead by the glory of the Father, even so we also should walk in newness of life" (Rom. 6:3–4).

Did you see it? That "we too may live a new life." See, eternal life doesn't begin when we die and go to heaven. It begins the moment Christ makes our spirit alive—we make a commitment to follow Him and trust Him to save us—and it continues forever. "Most assuredly, I say to you, he who hears My word and believes in Him who sent Me has everlasting life, and shall not come into judgment, but has passed from death into life" (John 5:24).

The Christian life is not a matter of dos and don'ts. It is a living, breathing relationship with Jesus Christ, with God Himself. It is about life—today, tomorrow, forever.

In John 10:10 Christ asserts, "I have come that they may have life, and that they may have it more abundantly."

In closing, let's summarize what we have studied in this last section.

✧ The cross is about death and about life.

- ✧ Jesus lived the perfect life, became the perfect sacrifice, was the perfect substitute for us. He paid the death penalty for all our sin.

- ✧ When Christ died, we died with Him.

- ✧ When Christ rose from the dead, He gave us new life

- ✧ At the moment of salvation, we pass from death to life.

- ✧ Eternal life begins at the moment of conversion/commitment and lasts forever.

Based on everything you have studied in this chapter, what are some of your thoughts? _____

_____

_____

_____

_____

_____

Okay, it is decision time. There are only two choices: say yes to Jesus, or say no to Jesus. Not to decide is a decision in itself.

Are you ready and willing to trust Jesus for your salvation and commit your life to following Him? If yes, then pray and ask Him to be your personal Lord and Savior. Record your prayer here: _____

_____

_____

_____

_____

_____

_____

_____

If you have more questions, record them here and seek out someone (a pastor or a friend who is a believer) to help you answer them: _____

_____

_____

_____

Application Questions

1. What one or two statements impacted me from this chapter?

   a. _____

   b. _____

2. How can I apply it/them to my life today and begin to pursue positive growth? _____
   _____

3. What one step am I willing to take to move toward heart change in my reactions, behavior or attitude? _____
   _____

4. What do I learn about God from this chapter? _____
   _____

5. How does His Word (the Bible) confirm this? _____
   _____
   _____

2

The Sufficiency of Your Sword

by Diane Hunt

Take the helmet of salvation and the sword of the Spirit, which is the word of God.

Ephesians 6:17

2

Regardless of where you currently find yourself, the Scriptures have a powerful message for you to give you hope, help and healing. God is in the business of transforming lives, and He uses His Word to do it. This chapter will take you on a brief journey through the Scriptures to impress upon you the power and sufficiency of the Bible to support you in the midst of your circumstances.

Real, abundant life comes from God and His Word, not earthly things. "So He humbled you, allowed you to hunger, and fed you with manna which you did not know nor did your fathers know, that He might make you know that man shall not live by bread alone; but man lives by every word that proceeds from the mouth of the Lord" (Deut. 8:3).

What is something you think could make your current situation better? What do you want most right now? _____

_____

Fill in the blank with your answer from above: "[I] shall not live by _____ alone but by every word that proceeds from the mouth of the Lord."

So if you said that you want security, then the quote would read "[I] shall not live by security alone, but by every word that proceeds from the mouth of the Lord." Perhaps what you want right now is a good father for your children; then it would read "[I] shall not live by having a good father for my children alone, but on every word that proceeds from the mouth of the Lord."

Your Heavenly Father provides everything you need for a complete, full life. Second Peter 1:3–4 tells us, "His divine power has given to us all things that pertain to life and godliness, through the knowledge of Him who called us by glory and virtue, by which have been given to us exceedingly great and precious promises, that through these you may be partakers of the divine nature, having escaped the corruption that is in the world through lust."

God has given us *all* things that pertain to life and godliness. This verse makes it clear that all our counsel should come from the Bible—not psychology or a watered-down version of the Bible mixed with psychology. Psalm 1:1–2 reminds us that we're blessed when we love and follow God's commands only:

> Blessed is the man
>> Who walks not in the counsel of the ungodly,
>> Nor stands in the path of sinners,
>> Nor sits in the seat of the scornful;

But his delight is in the law of the LORD,
And in His law he meditates day and night.

This verse cautions against seeking the ungodly counsel of the world, and any counsel that is not rooted in the Person and Word of God is ungodly. We are all taking counsel from somewhere; be careful to whom you are listening.

God desires for you to rely on Him more than any other person or thing in your life. The Lord will sustain you, and He keeps His promises, every single one. "Blessed be the LORD, who has given rest to His people Israel, according to all that He promised. There has not failed one word of all His good promise, which He promised through His servant Moses" (1 Kings 8:56). That is unique to God alone—not one of His promises has ever, nor will ever, fail. You can stand firm on them.

By trusting God's Word you can walk in a way removed from the world's temptations and pitfalls. Write Psalm 17:4: _____
_____
_____
_____

In what ways have you been deceived and beaten down? _____
_____
_____
_____
_____

What fears are keeping you from fully trusting God's Word? _____
_____
_____
_____
_____
_____

The Lord's Word will never fail. "For the word of the LORD is right, and all His work is done in truth" (Ps. 33:4). When you obey the Scripture, you can be confident that you are living truthfully and rightly. Biblical truth saves you from going down the wrong path. Psalm 107:20 tells us, "He sent His word and healed them, and delivered them from their destructions."

We are to take pleasure in reading God's Word; Psalm 119 offers an excellent picture of the psalmist's delight in Scripture. Take about fifteen minutes and read Psalm 119 in its entirety.

Now we're going to look at about twenty-five verses at a time. Read each section of verses and underline and count the number of words you find that have the same meaning as God's Word (word, law, testimonies, precepts, statutes, commandments, judgments, etc.). At the same time count each occurrence of the word "heart," and draw a heart by the verse it appears in.

	Occurrences of "word"	Occurrences of "heart"
Verses 1–24		
Verses 25–48		
Verses 49–72		
Verses 73–96		
Verses 97–128		
Verses 129–152		
Verses 153–176		
Total		

Reread Psalm 119:1–8.

Verses 1 and 2 say that those who walk in the law of the Lord and keep His testimonies are _____. How are we to seek Him? _____
_____

How are we to keep His precepts (119: 4)? _____

Verse 7 says, "I will praise You with uprightness of heart." How would you describe an upright heart?
_____
_____

Our hearts should be straight and true; we often find ourselves distracted by many things, things that seemingly demand our attention, but the words used to describe how we are to seek God (with the whole heart, diligently) indicate focused attention.

Reread Psalm 119:9–16. What is a powerful, practical tool we can use to keep from sinning (119:11)? ___
_____
_____

Not only should we memorize Scripture, but we should also _____ (119:15) and _____ on God's Word, precepts and ways. "But His delight is in the law of the LORD, and in His law he meditates day and night" (1:2). What does it mean to meditate (or focus on and ponder over) the Word of God? _____
_____
_____

Do you meditate on Scripture? How does it impact you? _____
_____
_____

Reread Psalm 119:17–24. According to verse 21, what does God call those who stray from His commandments? _____
_____

Why would a person who does not stay in and follow the Word be considered proud? _____
_____
_____

Verse 24 says, "Your testimonies also are my delight and my counselors." How does God's Word counsel you? _____

Reread Psalm 119:25–32.

What does the psalmist ask God to do in verse 25? _____
_____

What does a person's condition look like when he/she is in need of reviving/saving? _____
_____

Do you feel like you need to be revived/saved? In what way? _____
_____

What is another thing the psalmist asks God to do according to His Word (119:28)? _____
_____

Verse 31 says, "I cling to Your testimonies; O LORD, do not put me to shame!" How does one cling to God's testimonies? _____
_____
_____

When I think of clinging to someone or something, I think of having an urgent tenacity to hang on as if my life depended on it. That is, in a very real sense, exactly what it means to cling to God's Word—your life does depend on it.

Reread Psalm 119: 33–40.

It is easy to be distracted by what *seems* important—yet actually pales in comparison to God's best. That which distracts our attention often becomes an idol (a false object of devotion and worship) that draws us away from the Lord. Verse 37 says, "Turn away my eyes from looking at worthless things, and revive me in Your way."

What God is calling you to do is not just to add Him to your life but to turn away from that which has drawn you away from Him. God does not just want to be part of your life; God wants to be your life. As Paul writes, "For to me, to live is Christ" (Phil. 1:21).

When you turn your heart and life over to Christ, He fills you and lives through you. "I have been crucified with Christ; it is no longer I who live, but Christ lives in me" (Gal. 2:20).

We often desperately try to cling to what we want (godly husband, obedient children, financial stability, etc.) and grab on to Christ too. But Scripture says we are to cling to God's Word and, in so doing, to turn away from that which divides our heart: "Teach me Your way, O LORD, and I will walk in your truth; give me an undivided heart, that I may fear your name" (Ps. 86:11, NIV).

An undivided heart. In verse 37 the order is to turn your eyes from "worthless things" so you can experience revival. God desires to revive you, but not when you insist on keeping your eyes on your heart's desire. What will you cling to? _____

Reread Psalm 119:41–48. Salvation is a word that has several nuances in meaning. Verse 41 reads, "Let Your mercies come also to me, O LORD—Your salvation according to Your word." This occurrence of "salvation" is the Hebrew word for "safety or ease."

According to what does God grant salvation? (119:41) _____
_____

There really is power in the Word. It is the greatest resource for strength and change.

Reread Psalm 119:49–56. What does the Word of God offer? _____
_____

God is the God of all comfort who reveals Himself through His Word. "Blessed be the God and Father of our Lord Jesus Christ, the Father of mercies and God of all comfort, who comforts us in all our tribulation, that we may be able to comfort those who are in any trouble, with the comfort with which we ourselves are comforted by God" (2 Cor. 1:3–4).

Psalm 119:50 says, "Your word has given me life." In the King James Version, this verse is translated, "Thy word hath quickened me." "Quickened" carries several meanings: to revive, keep alive, give/promise life, nourish up, preserve, recover, repair, restore to life, be whole.[1] That is a serious statement about the power of the Word and its implications for your life.

Reread Psalm 119:57–64. What does it mean that God is your portion? _____
_____

In what ways does the truth that God is your portion impact your thinking about your situation? ____
_____
_____

Reread Psalm 119:65–72. How does God deal with us (119:65)? _____
_____
_____

What good comes out of affliction (119:67, 71)? _____
_____

Verse 72 proclaims, "The law of Your mouth is better to me than thousands of coins of gold and silver." What value would you place on God's Word? How much would you trade to have it? _____

_____

Reread Psalm 119:73–80. What did God do that gives Him more insight and knowledge about your life and what you need than any other living human being (119:73)? _____

_____

Why does the psalmist desire to be blameless before God (119:80)? _____

_____

When you stand before God, you will give an account. "But I say to you that for every idle word men may speak, they will give account of it in the day of judgment" (Matt. 12:36). "So then each of us shall give account of himself to God" (Rom. 14:12). "And there is no creature hidden from His sight, but all things are naked and open to the eyes of Him to whom we must give account" (Heb. 4:13). I don't know about you, but when I must give an account, I want to be blameless.

Reread Psalm 119:81–88. What was the author's complaint about the persecution he faced (119:85, 86)? _____

_____

In today's lingo, he's essentially saying he was treated unfairly. Can you identify with that? In what ways are you treated unfairly? _____

_____

How should you respond? _____

_____

> For this is commendable, if because of conscience toward God one endures grief suffering wrongfully. For what credit is it if when you are beaten for your faults, you take it patiently? But when you do good and suffer, if you take it patiently, this is commendable before God. For to this you were called, because Christ also suffered for us, leaving us an example, that you should follow His steps: 'Who committed no sin, nor was deceit found in His mouth'; who, when He was reviled, did not revile in return; when He suffered, He did not threaten, but committed Himself to Him who judges righteously; who Himself bore our sins in His own body on the tree, that we, having died to sins, might live for righteousness—by whose stripes you were healed. (1 Pet. 2:19–24)

Yes, your circumstances may be unfair, but in the midst of them, you are called to righteousness. God will never put you in a position in which you must sin. You will always have the choice to do the right thing. "No temptation has overtaken you except such as is common to man; but God is faithful, who will not allow you to be tempted beyond what you are able, but with the temptation will also make the way of escape, that you may be able to bear it" (1 Cor. 10:13).

Reread Psalm 119:89–96. What does this verse 92 tell you about your need to be in God's Word? ___

_____

_____

_____

Reread Psalm 119:97–104. Verse 101 says, "I have restrained my feet from every evil way, that I may keep Your word." When you think of restraining your feet, what thoughts come to mind? _____

_____

What was the psalmist's motivation? _____

_____

Verse 102 reads, "I have not departed from Your judgments, for You Yourself have taught me." How does God teach you, and what does He use? _____

_____

_____

Reread Psalm 119:107–112.

Do you, like the psalmist, feel greatly distressed? (Verse 107 says, "I am afflicted very much; Revive me, O Lord, according to Your word.") If so, why? _____

_____

_____

Where will you find your hope, help and healing? _____

Nine different times in Psalm 119, the psalmist asks God to revive him. Let's look at how he asks God to do it.

119:25	"Revive me according to Your _____."
119:37	"Revive me in Your _____."
119:40	"Revive me in Your _____."
119:88	"Revive me according to Your _____."
119:107	"Revive me, O Lord, according to Your _____."
119:149	"Revive me, according to Your _____."
119:154	"Revive me according to Your _____."
119:156	"Revive me according to Your _____."
119:159	"Revive me, O Lord, according to Your _____."

Do you desire to be revived? _____

In what areas of your life do you desire to be revived? _____

_____

How do you cry out to God for revival in your life? _____

_____

Reread Psalm 119:113–128. Have you ever felt like running away from your life ? Given that option, where would you go and why? _____

_____

_____

Does God being your hiding place bring peace to your heart? Why or why not? _____

_____

_____

Do you fear the judgment of God? Why or why not? _____

_____

_____

Is there anything you potentially love more than God? What is it? _____

_____

Reread Psalm 119:129–136.

Do you think you need to be educated or especially intelligent to understand the Scriptures? Why or why not? _____

Write Psalm 119:130: _____

_____

_____

How do you make decisions? What determines the course you chose? _____

_____

What does the psalmist ask God to do in verse 133? What does it mean to have your steps directed?

_____

_____

Are you allowing God to control your every step to keep you from sin? Reread Psalm 119:137–144. Do you usually associate commands with delight? What would it look like to take pleasure in God's laws? _____

_____

_____

Do you believe God's way is the only right way? _____

Reread Psalm 119:145–152. Verse 148 reads, "My eyes are awake through the night watches, that I may meditate on Your word."

When was the last time you could not sleep? _____

What was troubling you? _____

_____

_____

The psalmist doesn't sound like a man that read his Bible five minutes a day or a few times a month. His absolute delight in God and His Word overflows, and he was so committed to the Word of God that he lost sleep over it. Do you take the promises of God's Word equally seriously? How can you be like the psalmist—steeped in the Word and longing to meditate on God's truths? _____

_____

_____

Reread Psalm 119:153–160. Some people are willing to believe some of God's Word but not all of it, yet Psalm 119:160 says, "The entirety of Your word is truth, And every one of Your righteous judgments endures forever." *Every word is true.*

Do you believe God's Word is true in its entirety? If not, why not? _____

_____

From your knowledge of God and the Bible, which parts of His Word do you struggle with the most?

_____

Reread Psalm 119:161–168. Verse 165 says, "Great peace have those who love Your law, and nothing causes them to stumble." Have you ever stumbled in your Christian walk? What is your reaction to the promise that you will find peace when you love God's law? _____

_____

_____

_____

Reread Psalm 119:169–176.

Which verse encourages you the most? Why? _____

_____

_____

_____

Which verse challenges you the most? Why? _____

_____

_____

Have you ever intentionally praised God—even when you don't feel like it? What was the result? ___

_____

When you sin, are you more upset over the consequences or because your sin offends God? _____

_____

I started this chapter by saying you have available to you the ultimate resource for personal change. How has your attitude about the Scriptures changed? _____

_____

_____

_____

Do you believe the Word of God is a powerful instrument of change for your life? _____

_____

What would you like God to change about you, not your circumstances, not others, but you? _____

_____

_____

The Word of God is vital to our healing, hope and peace. Consider Hebrews 4:12: "For the word of God is living and powerful, and sharper than any two-edged sword, piercing even to the division of soul and spirit, and of joints and marrow, and is a discerner of the thoughts and intents of the heart."

What does it mean to you personally to have access to the Word of God? _____

_____

The Word of God is living and active. If you find the Bible dull and boring, consider:

> 1) In order to properly grasp the Bible's message, you need to be spiritually discerning. In other words, without the Holy Spirit residing in you through the regeneration of your spirit, the Scriptures will simply be a literary pursuit, not a spiritual one. "These things we also speak, not in words which man's wisdom teaches but which the Holy Spirit teaches, comparing spiritual things with spiritual. But the natural man does not receive the things of the Spirit of God, for they are foolishness to him; nor can he know them, because they are spiritually discerned" (1 Cor. 2:13–14).

> 2) Perhaps you are reading other things that draw your heart and mind away from the truth. Are you dulling your sensitivity to the Word of God with distracting things such as romance novels, television or Christian-fluff (books or programs that carry the "Christian" label but are not deeply rooted in God's Word) that are more interested in making you feel better than challenging you with truth?

Remember, the Word of God is like a healing balm for a tired and weary soul. It speaks life where sickness and death reign. "Remember the Word to Your servant, upon which You have caused me to hope. This is my comfort in my affliction, for Your Word has given me life" (Ps.119:49–50).

In Psalm 81:10, the Lord declares, "Open your mouth wide, and I will fill it." Open your mouth wide and take a long satisfying drink of the Living Water. Immerse yourself in the Word of the Lord and find yourself refreshed in the deepest part of your soul.

Application Questions

1. What one or two statements impacted me from this chapter?

   a. _____

   b. _____

2. How can I apply it/them to my life today and begin to pursue positive growth? _____

   _____

3. What one step am I willing to take to move toward heart change in my reactions, behavior or attitude? _____

   _____

4. What do I learn about God from this chapter? _____

   _____

5. How does His Word (the Bible) confirm this? _____

   _____

   _____

3

Suffering: A Tool in God's Hand

by Diane Hunt

So then, those who suffer according to God's will should commit themselves to their faithful Creator and continue to do good.

1 Peter 4:19

3

*I*f you are reading this Bible study, chances are that you are experiencing or have experienced suffering, perhaps in the form of:

- ✧ Financial debt
- ✧ Relational discord
- ✧ Infidelity
- ✧ Sexually-transmitted disease
- ✧ Parenting problems
- ✧ Abuse
- ✧ A damaged reputation
- ✧ Living situations
- ✧ Dangerous liaisons

What consequences are you personally dealing with, from the list or not, which add to your suffering?

_____

_____

There is no doubt that you have been sinned against if you are in a relationship with a person trapped in addiction, but we must not stop there. If we did, we would end up with a hopeless, discouraging, dark view of life. Although you have been sinned against, guard against having a victim mentality, believing that you are the way you are because of what someone else has done. If he/she changes, then you can change. And, that once he/she changes, then you can be okay, happy, content, whatever. Through this way of thinking, you give a great deal of power and control to the other person. Your happiness and contentment are rooted in another individual. If he/she never changes, you can never be happy.

What robs you of happiness or contentment? _____

_____

_____

_____

_____

_____

If you could change three things about your life, what would they be, and why would you change them? _____

_____

_____

_____

How is your life perspective impacted by others? _____

_____

_____

With the immensity of the problem and ramifications of addiction, it is easy to discount or minimize our own sin. Part of our goal is to get your eyes off the other person's sin (which you cannot change), and get your eyes onto yourself.

Consider this statement: "The cause of my struggle is not the people or the situation in my life, but the 'heart' that I bring to those relationships and circumstances."[1] In other words, it is not what is outside of you that is causing your problems; it is what is inside of you reacting to what is outside of you. What are your thoughts about this statement? _____

_____

_____

_____

Do you struggle to accept that you are responsible for your attitude and actions regardless of what other people do or say? Why or why not? _____

_____

_____

_____

It is important to realize that you are not only the offended but also an offender. First and foremost, you are an offender against God and second, an offender against others. You may find that hard to swallow, but consider this: every time you failed to respond to another person in a godly manner, regardless of his behavior, you have offended God and sinned against the other individual. I know that is painfully difficult to accept, but acceptance of this truth is a necessary step on your path to freedom.

Read Matthew 18: 21–35. What is the overall message of this parable? _____

_____

_____

_____

_____

Why was the master angry (18:32–33)? _____

_____

_____

_____

What is the command God gives to each of us in verse 35? _____

_____

_____

_____

You are not a hopeless victim. You have options. You can be obedient, holy and righteous in your situation. "I can do all things through Christ who strengthens me" (Phil. 4:13). Christ will give you the power to live according to His will, even when you feel completely beaten down. "And He said to me, 'My grace is sufficient for you, for My power is made perfect in weakness'" (2 Cor. 12:9).

That said, I understand that you are suffering. I don't want to downplay the seriousness of your situation; I just want to help you gain biblical perspective in the midst of your suffering. The Bible has a lot to say about persevering through tribulations.

First, we should expect suffering to be part of our experience as believers. John 16:33 tells us, "These things I have spoken to you, that in Me you may have peace. In the world you will have tribulation; but be of good cheer, I have overcome the world."

The first part of the sentence uses the verb "will have." That sounds pretty definite, doesn't it? It does not say you *may* have or *if* you have; it says you *will have* tribulation.

Suffering has a purpose. Remember that God is sovereign and orchestrates each life to accomplish His purposes. "Beloved, do not think it strange concerning the fiery trail which is to try you, as though some strange thing happened to you; but rejoice to the extent that you partake of Christ's suffering, that when His glory is revealed, you may also be glad with exceeding joy. . . . Therefore, let those who suffer according to the will of God commit their souls to Him in doing good as to a faithful Creator" (1 Pet.4:12–13, 19).

God works *all* things according to the counsel of His will. "In Him also we have obtained an inheritance, being predestined according to the purpose of Him who works all things according to the counsel of His will, that we who first trusted in Christ should be to the praise of His glory" (Eph. 1:11–12).

In the booklet "The Four Spiritual Laws," the first spiritual law is "God loves you and offers a wonderful plan for your life."[2] The truth is that that wonderful plan for your life includes suffering. You see, God has a purpose for your affliction and a plan to help you persevere.

You *can* persevere as a woman of character, filled with hope:

> Therefore, having been justified by faith, we have peace with God through our Lord Jesus Christ, through whom also we have access by faith into this grace in which we stand, and rejoice in hope of the glory of God. And not only that, but we also glory in tribulations, knowing that tribulation produces perseverance; and perseverance, character; and character, hope. Now hope does not disappoint, because the love of God has been poured out in our hearts by the Holy Spirit who was given to us. (Rom. 5:1–5)

No matter what you face, the Holy Spirit will be with you and will give you patience. James 1:2–4 tells us, "My brethren, count it all joy when you fall into various trials, knowing that the testing of your faith produces patience. But let patience have its perfect work, that you may be perfect and complete, lacking nothing."

Remember, we are looking at what Scripture has to say about the purpose of suffering. "Only let your conduct be worthy of the gospel of Christ, so that whether I come and see you or am absent, I may hear of your affairs, that you stand fast in one spirit, with one mind striving together for the faith of the gospel, and not in any way terrified by your adversaries, which is to them a proof of perdition, but to you of salvation, and that from God. For to you it has been granted on behalf of Christ, not only to believe in Him, but also to suffer for His sake, having the same conflict which you saw in me and now hear is in me" (Phil. 1:27–30).

One goal is to suffer for Christ's sake. It says, "For to you it has been granted on behalf of Christ . . ." Philippians makes facing tribulations sound like an honor.

Paul offers us a strong example of giving up all things to follow Christ:

> But what things were gain to me, these I have counted loss for Christ. Yet indeed I also count all things loss for the excellence of the knowledge of Christ Jesus my Lord, for whom I have suffered the loss of all things, and count them as rubbish, that I may gain Christ and be found in Him, not having my own righteousness, which is from the law, but that which is through faith in Christ, the righteousness which is from God by faith; that I may know Him and the power of His resurrection, and the fellowship of His sufferings, being conformed to His death, if by any means, I may attain to the resurrection from the dead. (Phil. 3:7–11)

Although there were things that were important to Paul, what was most important to him? _____
_____

Paul gave up all things that he might _____ Christ. He desired to know Christ and the _____ of His _____ and the _____ of His _____.

What have you suffered the loss of? _____

Please do not think we are minimizing your loss. Loss is loss. It is painful. We understand the pain of loss. We are sorry for the loss you have experienced in your life. But which would you rather have: more of Christ or what you have lost?

Your loss has purpose if through it you grow in your relationship with Jesus Christ. You will not walk in freedom if you focus on what you have lost in life rather than what you gain in Christ. Your loss and suffering have a purpose—that you may gain something far greater.

Suffering is a learning opportunity. Christ learned obedience through suffering. "Though He was a Son, yet He learned obedience by the things which He suffered" (Heb. 5:8). The Scripture says He was made perfect through suffering. "For it was fitting for Him, for whom are all things and by whom are all things, in bringing many sons to glory, to make the captain of their salvation perfect through sufferings" (Heb. 2:10).

Christ is the captain of our salvation. It was He who was made perfect through suffering—tried and tested and found to be true. In His suffering He "committed no sin, nor was deceit found in His mouth" (1 Pet. 2:22). We have an example in our suffering—a knowing and compassionate Lord. Let's look at First Peter 2:21–23 in its entirety: "For to this you were called, because Christ also suffered for us, leaving us an example, that you should follow His steps: 'Who committed no sin, nor was deceit found in His mouth'; who, when He was reviled, did not revile in return; when He suffered, He did not threaten, but committed Himself to Him who judges righteously."

What guidelines should we follow from Christ's example? _____
_____
_____

So what is your calling? Let's go back just a few verses: "Servants, be submissive to your masters with all fear, not only to the good and gentle, but also to the harsh. For this is commendable, if because of conscience toward God one endures grief, suffering wrongfully. For what credit is it if when you are beaten for your faults, you take it patiently? But when you do good and suffer, if you take it patiently, this is commendable before God" (1 Pet. 2:18–20).

How can you commit your specific situation to Him who judges righteously? _____
_____

Remember, Christ has experienced hurt, pain and suffering. He understands. "For we do not have a High Priest who cannot sympathize with our weaknesses, but was in all points tempted as we are, yet without sin" (Heb. 4:15). He is a compassionate and loving Lord, and we are to be patient and good-willed, suffering for His cause.

Understanding suffering from the biblical perspective lightens our load—but it does not remove our pain. Pray and ask God to put your suffering in perspective and to give you understanding and acceptance. Ask that you may see the supreme value of gaining Christ.

Additional Resources

Why? by Anne Graham Lotz

A Path Through Suffering by Elisabeth Elliot

Suffering and the Sovereignty of God edited by John Piper and Justin Taylor

Suffering: Eternity Makes a Difference by Paul David Tripp

Application Questions

1. What one or two statements impacted me from this chapter?

    a. _____

    b. _____

2. How can I apply it/them to my life today and begin to pursue positive growth? _____
    _____

3. What one step am I willing to take to move toward heart change in my reactions, behavior or attitude? _____
    _____

4. What do I learn about God from this chapter? _____
    _____

5. How does His Word (the Bible) confirm this? _____
    _____
    _____

4

Addiction: Idols of the Heart

by Diane Hunt and Stephanie Paul

For God alone, O my soul, wait in silence,
for my hope is from him.
He only is my rock and my salvation,
my fortress; I shall not be shaken.
On God rests my salvation and my glory;
my mighty rock, my refuge is God.

Trust in him at all times, O people;
pour out your heart before him;
God is a refuge for us.   Selah

Psalm 62:5–8 (ESV)

4

Addiction can be a scary and somewhat confusing topic. Perhaps your husband or fiancé, your son or daughter, or you struggle with life-dominating temptations.

We tend to think of addiction as having to do with sex, drugs, alcohol or gambling; and while, these are, humanly speaking, the most typical destructive addictions, they are by no means the only addictions our society struggles with. In this chapter we hope to broaden your thinking to see addiction and idolatry as synonymous, and we hope you gain a greater understanding of the roots of addiction—even to see the ones that have been firmly planted in your own heart.

The world tends to define addiction as a disease. By definition disease is "a pathological condition of a body part, an organ, or a system resulting from various causes, such as infection, genetic defect or environmental stress, and characterized by an identifiable group of signs or symptoms."[1] The American Medical Association classifies addiction as a disease, and this view, held by a vast majority, is taught in most secular rehabs and support groups such as AA, NA, etc.

An alternative, biblical view of addiction is grace-based rather than disease-based. You see, the answer to addiction is not a method but rather a Savior. If addiction is a disease, there is little hope of a cure, and the best a person can do is learn to cope. This "coping" attitude tends to minimize responsibility for one's own behavior and the devastation it causes. As we take a deeper look at the Bible, we believe you will find Scripture's perspective to be filled with hope.

The Bible refers to addiction not as sickness but rather as sin. The world may have you believe that it's simply a "condition," but God's Word warns us not to be deceived:

> Be careful, or your hearts will be weighed down with dissipation, drunkenness and the anxieties of life, and that day will close on you unexpectedly like a trap. (Luke 21:34, NIV)

> Let us behave decently, as in the daytime, not in orgies and drunkenness, not in sexual immorality and debauchery, not in dissension and jealousy. (Rom.13:13, NIV)

> For you have spent enough time in the past doing what pagans choose to do—living in debauchery, lust, drunkenness, orgies, carousing and detestable idolatry. (1 Pet. 4:3, NIV)

When you consider that disease is something with a small chance of a cure, there is little hope. If addiction is understood as life-dominating sin, however, there is great hope, because we have a Savior who forgives sin and who offers unending grace (mercy, pardon, favor). There is hope in speaking and applying the words of Scripture to addiction or any other sin.

Write the following Scriptures:

First John 1:9 _____

_____

Hebrews 4:16 _____

_____

Romans 15:13 _____

_____

When I (Stephanie) used to think of an "addict," the picture that always came to my mind was that of a junkie—you know, some dude on the street, strung out on drugs. The "addict" never ever had my husband's face. Over time my thinking has been challenged, and I have been stretched and grown as a result. I have come face to face with the reality of the "reckless nature of the human heart."[2] The Word of God provides rich answers to our fallen humanness; our "cure" stems from being self-controlled, through the empowerment of the Holy Spirit and through obedience to God's rule in and over our lives. From the very beginning Scripture causes us over and over again to see our huge need for help. We must embrace and accept the Christ of Scripture as our best and only answer.

Although our focus in addiction is primarily on drugs and alcohol, addiction covers all kinds of sins that are not easily cast off. The following definition of addiction is offered by Dr. Edward Welch, considered to be an expert in the field of addictions: "Addiction is defined as bondage to the rule of a substance, activity, or state of mind, which then becomes the center of life, *defending itself from the truth* so that even bad consequences don't bring repentance and lead to further estrangement from God."[3]

Can you think of anything in your life that might fit into this definition? _____

_____

As the wife of a former addict, I can testify to the truth that my husband's drug of choice became the "center of life" at various times, for different lengths of time, which for me produced the worst feelings I'd ever experienced. In those times nothing and no one mattered more to my husband than being high.

No addict ever sets out to be consumed and destroyed. Addiction's false promise that you'll feel better or escape your problems, etc. becomes "truth," and truth becomes something that is doubted and mistrusted rather than the very thing that we cling to for life.

As you seek the Christ of Scripture, you will see that for you and the person in your life struggling in addiction, there is no other way to overcome the battle and live in freedom. All of us, without exception, must take our soul to task. In other words, we must utterly destroy the idols of our heart. (Read Ezek. 14:3–6).

On top of being sin, addiction is also a form of bondage. Dr. Welch refers to it as voluntary slavery. That almost sounds like an oxymoron, yet it captures the double-edged blade of addiction. Lest we who don't consider ourselves addicts feel too comfortable, consider what addiction really is—idolatry. We started this chapter saying "we hope to broaden your thinking to see addiction and idolatry as synonymous."

Dr. Welch's definition of addiction begins with the phrase "bondage to the rule of . . ." When we are in bondage to the rule of anything or anyone other than God we are sinning against Him. Likewise, idolatry is worshiping anything or anyone other than the one true God.

Idolatry, according to *Easton's Bible Dictionary*, is "image-worship or divine honor paid to any created object."[4] An idol can be anything or anyone that interferes with, distracts you from or replaces your relationship with God. It's a matter of misplaced worship.

Webster's Dictionary defines idolatry as "blind or excessive devotion to something."[5] We are born worshipers. We will all worship someone or something; it is simply a matter of whom or what we will worship.

I cringe to think of myself as an addict, but if I apply the above definition to myself, I must be. My addiction is to food. No way did I ever think food would consume so much space in my life—especially since food is, in moderation, a good thing. The bad consequences of over sixty extra pounds of body weight (most of which is fat) have not led me to stop eating more food than is necessary for living a healthy life. I am and have been sorry, but that guilty sorrow has not led to godly sorrow (repentance) and change. Why? Because the bodily experience provided by eating feels good—at least at the moment. The answer is simple, yet the struggle is not so easy to overcome. My battle has given me a greater depth of compassion for those who are bound by other substances. Oh, that we would sorrow over sin and eagerly repent to free ourselves from bondage! May it be so, in Jesus' name!

Who or what demands the majority of your attention, energy or devotion? _____
_____
_____

Where do you go to get your needs met? (Think especially about those activities that provide some kind of experience in our bodies or that meet a bodily need.) _____
_____

Where/how do you find comfort from stress? _____
_____
_____

You may be beginning to see that you are not much different than the addicted person in your life. Your "object of worship" may just be different, more socially acceptable than theirs. You may be feeling sorry over your own sin. Repentance for our sins is born out of a form of godly sorrow—of having a contrite spirit before God.

In Second Corinthians 7:8–11, Paul writes,

> Even if I caused you sorrow by my letter, I do not regret it. Though I did regret it—I see that my letter hurt you, but only for a little while—yet now I am happy, not because you were made sorry, but because your sorrow led you to repentance. For you became sorrowful as God intended and so were not harmed in any way by us. Godly sorrow brings repentance that leads to salvation and leaves no regret, but worldly sorrow brings death. See what this godly sorrow has produced in you: what earnestness, what eagerness to clear yourselves, what indignation, what alarm, what longing, what concern, what readiness to see justice done. At every point you have proved yourselves to be innocent in this matter. (NIV)

I like the way this verse reads in *The Message*. Beginning at verse 10 and ending at 13, this paraphrased version reads,

> Distress that drives us to God does that. It turns us around. It gets us back in the way of salvation. We never regret that kind of pain. But those who let distress drive them away from God are full of regrets, end up on a deathbed of regrets. And now, isn't it wonderful all the ways in which this distress has goaded you closer to God? You're more alive, more concerned, more sensitive, more reverent, more human, more passionate, more responsible. Looked at from any angle, you've come out of this with purity of heart. And that is what I was hoping for in the first place when I wrote the letter. My primary concern was not for the one who did the wrong or even the one wronged, but for you—that you would realize and act upon the deep, deep ties between us before God.

God of mercy and hope, God of our salvation, may we even now, realize and act upon what we have read from Your Word. May our hearts be moved beyond surface sorrow into godly sorrow that leaves us longing, panting, yearning and then acting upon the deep ties between You and us. Amen

A few questions to pause and ponder:

Where do you go and what do you do when you need to feel in control? _____
_____
_____

Whom or what do you focus on? _____
_____
_____
_____

Who or what tends to control your time? _____
_____
_____
_____

What are you likely to do when you are down, depressed, worried or anxious? _____
_____
_____
_____

Whatever you wrote in the blanks is likely whom or what you are worshiping. Do you know you can worship or idolize something you hate? I think it would be safe to say that for every addict, there comes a point at which he detests the very thing he turns to for release, comfort, etc. Sometimes that hatred, anger and bitterness consumes us and becomes an idol.

Welch offers a list of addictive substances and desires but admits that addictions are virtually only limited by our own imaginations (we have made additions to his list in italics): *alcohol*, exercise, entertainment, anger, nose drops, *music*, sex, *thinness*, love, shoplifting, *spouse*, *romance novels*, caffeine, cocaine, sugar, television, risk, gambling, *nicotine*, people, weightlifting, sports, lying, *shopping*, work, chocolate, pornography, sleep, *friends*, *news*, pain, *children*, success/winning, etc.[6]

What are some examples of addiction in your own heart and life? What activities or substances entice you? Are there any areas in your life that you believe may fit into the category of "addiction" or "idols of your heart?" _____

_____

_____

_____

_____

_____

Look at Welch's list again. You may wonder how your children could possibly be seen as an addiction. Let me give a story to illustrate. Not too long after my husband graduated and left the Colony of Mercy at America's Keswick, I attended a Women of Character support group meeting. During the meeting, as we shared our experiences with one another, one of the wives perfectly described how her children and family were, for her, an addiction or "an idol of her heart." She said, "Nothing matters more than my kids and having a perfect family. As long as my family is doing well, then all is well with me." Her well-being, her peace and her reason for being were totally dependent on her kids. Something other than Christ had become the "center of life" for her. Her words paraphrased were, "All I ever wanted was to be a mom and to have a family. What's wrong with that?!"

Was her desire for love wrong? Surely not! But putting her children first in her life and turning to them for everything, expecting them to fill a gap in her heart, put God in last place. Matthew 6:33 tells us, "But seek first the Kingdom of God and his righteousness, and all these things will be added to you" (ESV). We must seek God first. To do anything else is sin. There is no other way to say it.

"For my people have committed two evils: they have forsaken Me, the fountain of living waters, and hewn themselves cisterns, broken cisterns that can hold no water" (Jer. 2:13).

When we move from worshiping the one true God with true heart devotion to "needing" some other thing, we have moved from godly worship to idolatry. Idolatry is a form of bondage that does not easily release its captive.

Praise God for the wife who shared so openly and honestly in that meeting. God had prepared her heart in advance to hear the gospel message, and she received Him as her Savior right then and there. For the first time she understood that Jesus wanted to be the one to fill that gap in her life. He was for her, and He was the only one who could satisfy her broken heart.

"God says, I am the only one that can meet your needs! When I'm sitting there saying, I would like to fill your heart with Myself and you forsake the living water, when I could satisfy and fill you up and then you go and do your own thing. He says, When I am holding out my hands to you and have what you need and you refuse to take it and it keeps sending you back to the same thing over and over again—that is sin."[7]

What is the inner longing of your soul that you thought your marriage would meet? _____

_____

_____

Is your inner longing peace? Is it security? Is it comfort and ease? Are you willing to get honest with yourself and God and confess any sin that is the result of trying to fill those longings? _____

Are you afraid to acknowledge to God what your addictions may be? Guess what? He already knows! What a relief that is. We just need to bring everything to Him and let go. "He [God] wants us to admit to it, so we will know and recognize it and keep from going back. Let's not stay in a state of denial. If we do we will stay in that same cycle. Once we decide to open our eyes to what it has cost us, we will decide."[8]

"O God, you are my God; earnestly I seek you; my soul thirsts for you; my flesh faints for you, as in a dry and weary land where there is no water. So I have looked upon you in the sanctuary, beholding your power and glory. Because your steadfast love is better than life, my lips will praise you. So I will bless you as long as I live; in your name I will lift up my hands. My soul will be satisfied as with fat and rich food, and my mouth will praise you with joyful lips, when I remember you upon my bed, and meditate on you in the watches of the night; for you have been my help, and in the shadow of your wings I will sing for joy. My soul clings to you; your right hand upholds me" (Ps. 63:1–8, ESV).

Adultery is a biblical metaphor that, in a sense, describes how addiction draws us away from the one true God. Ezekiel 16 is a graphic depiction of what God did for each of His children and what we tend to do in return. Read it, and as you read, fill in the following table:

What Did God Do?	What Did Jerusalem Do?
Ex. He made them thrive (16:7)	Trusted in their own beauty (16:15)

What do you think God was trying to communicate through Ezekiel (16:1–5)? _____

_____

_____

What do you think God is saying He did in response to our unwanted neglected spiritual state (16:6–14)? _____

_____

_____

Summarize what Jerusalem did in response (16:15–19). _____

_____

_____

_____

Essentially, God rescued us, saved us and made us part of His family, and we turned our back on Him and looked elsewhere for love, comfort, assurance and identity. We look to food, sex, drugs, husbands, children, exercise, the mall, friends, gambling, alcohol, prescription meds, etc. (see 16:20–26).

Ezekiel 16:32 speaks volumes: "You are an adulterous wife, who takes strangers instead of her husband." Isn't that what we essentially do when we turn to other people for comfort, or to food when we are anxious, or to TV when we are depressed? We numb our feelings or dull our minds, but it is never enough, is it? There is always the need to come back for more—unless our first step is to get on our knees and on our faces before the God of *all* comfort.

This is confirmed for us in Second Corinthians 1:3–5:

> Blessed be the God and Father of our Lord Jesus Christ, the Father of mercies and God of all comfort, who comforts us in all our tribulation, that we may be able to comfort those who are in any trouble, with the comfort with which we ourselves are comforted by God. For as the sufferings of Christ abound in us, so our consolation also abounds through Christ.

It's not that we shouldn't speak to our friends when we need comfort, but it shouldn't be the first place we go. First we need to go to our heavenly Husband—God.

What is the result of adultery, idolatry and addiction in Ezekiel 16:35–43? _____

_____

_____

_____

_____

This is a pretty sobering picture, and addictions and idolatry come in all shapes and sizes. We tend to think of idols as statues that people worship or speak to, but Ezekiel 14:1–11 gives us a little different perspective:

> Now some of the elders of Israel came to me and sat before me. And the word of the LORD came to me, saying, "Son of man, these men have set up their idols in their hearts, and put before them that which causes them to stumble into iniquity. Should I let Myself be inquired of at all by them?" Therefore, speak to them, and say to them, 'Thus says the Lord GOD; "Everyone of the house of Israel who sets up his idols in his heart, and puts before him what causes him to stumble into iniquity, and then comes to the prophet, I the LORD will answer him who comes, according to the multitude of his idols, that I may seize the house of Israel by their heart, because they all are estranged from Me by their idols.'"

Where did the men set up their idols? _____

What do these idols cause them to do? _____

How many idols does the Lord say they have? _____

How did these idols affect their relationship with God? _____
_____

Clearly, idolatry involves something more personal to us than stone statues and golden calves; it is as intimate as our own hearts.

We want to be sure that you fully understand the addiction/idol of the heart connection. Let's do a little exercise. Earlier we asked you to consider your own heart and life. Are there examples (from the chart) of addiction/idols of the heart that you can identify with? What were they? _____
_____
_____
_____

What do these "idols" cause you to do? _____
_____

How do these "idols" affect your relationship with others? _____
_____
_____

How do these "idols" affect your relationship with God? _____
_____
_____
_____

Here are a few illustrations of potential idols:

1. Work. In Genesis, we read that God created us to work the land, rule the land and help one another. I read an article online that said, "It is not surprising therefore, that in a fallen world we have turned work itself into a slave master and a god. Much of our cultural drivenness focuses around our longing for significance through professional accomplishments. Workaholics are chronically absorbed in a continuous stream of tasks. Their sense of well-being is wrapped up in what they do."[9]

2. Food. I'd be grossly remiss if I left this one off the list. I almost wonder if my good friend, mentor, co-worker and boss assigned me to write this chapter in the hope that I might glean insight that could turn into proactive application, which would ultimately result in lasting change and freedom. One look at me and my addiction is obvious. I am overweight—"obese" by medical definition because my body fat percentage is more than 30%. At present, my lifestyle supports my being overweight and staying overweight. It is this very thing—this seemingly insatiable appetite for food—that has enabled me to sympathize with the addicts with whom I interact. "With food some of us attempt to satisfy not only the natural need of our bodies but also in-

satiable emotional and spiritual longings. The more we eat to feel better, the more our bodies work with our emotions to increase the demand. The cycle is addictive."[10]

3. Relationships. How is it possible that we could become enslaved to another person? "We can develop an enslaving, destructive dependence on people. This form of idolatry occurs when we view another person as the source of our identity and well-being. Alone we feel empty, unfulfilled and helpless. When threatened with separation, we fight to cling to the other person at all cost, even to the harm of the one we claim to love."[11]

   You may identify this as co-dependency. Co-dependency is an addiction to another; it is when a person becomes your drug of choice. When relationship with that person, whether good or bad, is our focus in life, we become co-dependent—in other words, that person becomes an idol of our heart.

The bottom line of all addiction—all the idols of your heart—is that *instead of serving God, you serve yourself.*

By this point in the chapter, you have a stronger understanding of the what and the who of addiction. It's now time for true confession. Will the "real" addict please stand up? The truth is that everyone, in one way or another, struggles with some form of addiction.

To avoid finger-pointing and, worse yet, having a spirit of self-righteousness, we must look for addictions in our own heart and life. "We must always preach to ourselves, before we preach to others."[12] Thinking about your own struggles is often the best way to begin to understand and help the addict in your life. Notice I said "help"—not excuse, enable or equip.

Addictions are sins from which we can't easily escape. We can become "the slave of something, an activity or substance that entices us, which leaves us wanting to come back for more, even though more might not be wise or godly."[13] The only way to overcome our life-controlling sins is to place our trust in the One who can save and protect us:

> My soul, wait silently for God alone, for my expectation is from Him. He only is my rock and my salvation; He is my defense; I shall not be moved. In God is my salvation and my glory; the rock of my strength, And my refuge, is in God. Trust in Him at all times, you people; pour out your heart before Him; God is a refuge for us. Selah. (Ps.62:5–8)

The answer to all addiction, any and all idolatry, is to fall so in love with Jesus Christ that the things that hold you captive fade in comparison. And that isn't just some nice little statement I've contrived— His love is truly better than life!

Only when we have come to the end of own pursuit for relief or power, will we turn to God for freedom from the bondage of addiction.

Let us thirst after God in the same way David did when he was in the wilderness of Judah:

> O God, You are my God;
>   Early will I seek You;
>   My soul thirsts for You;

My flesh longs for You
    In a dry and thirsty land
    Where there is no water.
So I have looked for You in the sanctuary,
    To see Your power and Your glory.
Because Your lovingkindness is better than life,
    My lips shall praise You.
Thus I will bless You while I live;
    I will lift up my hands in Your name.
My soul shall be satisfied as with marrow and fatness,
    And my mouth shall praise You with joyful lips.
When I remember You on my bed,
    I meditate on You in the night watches.
Because You have been my help,
    Therefore in the shadow of Your wings I will rejoice. (Ps. 63:1–7)

Jesus, the true Lover of your soul, is eager to satisfy your longings. He is all you need, and He is everything you need. Will you trust Him to be your All in all? He proclaims, "Behold, I stand at the door and knock. If anyone hears My voice and opens the door, I will come in to him and dine with him, and he with Me" (Rev. 3:20).

Additional Resources

There is much more to be said concerning addiction. Here are several titles that I strongly encourage you to read so that your eyes may be opened to see the bigger picture of addiction:

Addictions: A Banquet in the Grave: Finding Hope in the Power of the Gospel by Edward T. Welch

Good News for the Chemically Dependent and Those Who Love Them by Jeff VanVonderen

When We Just Can't Stop by Tim Jackson and Jeff Olson (rbc.org)

Idols of the Heart: Learning to Long for God Alone by Elyse Fitzpatrick

Application Questions

1. What one or two statements impacted me from this chapter?

   a. _____

   b. _____

2. How can I apply it/them to my life today and begin to pursue positive growth? _____
   _____

3. What one step am I willing to take to move toward heart change in my reactions, behavior or attitude? _____
   _____

4. What do I learn about God from this chapter? _____
   _____

5. How does His Word (the Bible) confirm this? _____
   _____
   _____

5

Responding Biblically in the Midst of It

by Stephanie Paul

The fear of the LORD is the beginning of knowledge:
but fools despise wisdom and instruction.

Proverbs 1:7

For the LORD gives wisdom;
From His mouth come knowledge and understanding;
He stores up sound wisdom for the upright;
He is a shield to those who walk uprightly;
He guards the paths of justice,
And preserves the way of His saints.
Then you will understand righteousness and justice,
Equity and every good path.
When wisdom enters your heart,
And knowledge is pleasant to your soul,
Discretion will preserve you;
Understanding will keep you.

Proverbs 2:6–11

5

I have been where you are. By God's grace my life and marriage have been marvelously transformed in the crucible of addiction, pain and suffering. It is my prayer that through careful study of this chapter you will better understand that you matter to God and, therefore, that how you respond in situations matters to God. God wants you to know beyond the shadow of a doubt that you are loved. He wants you to know that He is with you now in the midst of whatever you are going through, and He will be with you always. You are His child; He is your Father.

I hope you will be encouraged to pursue God for more wisdom and understanding—for a deeper, more satisfying relationship with Him, and for a better way to respond in all life's situations—not just the ones related to addiction. It is the God of Abraham, Isaac and Jacob who will one day make plain to you the meaning behind every tear you have shed and any sorrow your heart has suffered.[1]

There are no promises or guarantees that you will *feel* better if you do everything that this chapter suggests. We're discussing a difficult topic that doesn't promise to leave you with any "warm fuzzies." But with absolute certainty, I can tell you this: if you seek the God of your salvation, you will find Him. In Him and Him alone (not your husband, fiancé, etc.) is your hope and your future; in Him you can feel better—and be better—inside; and in Him you will find strength and joy for each day.

You can know for certain that God is with you and for you. You can have the absolute joy of the Lord. This joy is such that you can, as the psalmist penned centuries ago, "Sing praise to the LORD, you saints of His, and give thanks at the remembrance of His holy name" (30:4). *The Message* paraphrases this verse as, "All you saints! Sing your heart out to God. Thank Him to His face."

"For I know the thoughts that I think toward you, says the LORD, thoughts of peace and not of evil, to give you a future and a hope. Then you will call upon Me and go and pray to Me, and I will listen to you. And you will seek Me and find Me, when you search for Me with all your heart. I will be found by you, says the LORD, and I will bring you back from your captivity; I will gather you from all the nations and from all the places where I have driven you, says the LORD, and I will bring you to the place from which I cause you to be carried away captive." (Jer. 29:11–13)

We are made up of body, soul and spirit—material and immaterial. Once we come to faith in Christ, a total change takes place. Our spirits are born anew; as our souls and our minds are renewed, we are transformed more and more into the image of Christ.

As we grow in faith, we are less compelled by our flesh to live self-centered lives. As time passes, we are more and more drawn by the Spirit to want to live according to our new nature in Christ. Our renewed spirits exert an irresistible pressure on us, and we turn from our old ways, drawn to "do life" as the Holy Spirit guides us.

Thus our journey begins toward a God-focused, Christ-centered, Holy Spirit-empowered life, through which we will bit by bit learn what it means to respond biblically (God's way) to life's situations.

Do you believe that every situation you will encounter has an answer in the Bible? _____ _____ If not, what kinds of situations don't you believe are addressed? _____ _____ _____

From your perspective, how does the Bible relate to everyday life? _____ _____ _____

What would a biblical response in your specific circumstance look like? How do you begin to think about biblically responding in your personal situation? _____ _____ _____ _____

Examining Our Hearts

We're often quick to see others as the source of our problems before examining our own hearts to see if we are the ones creating the problem. Jesus says that our sin is coming from our hearts—from inside us not from a source outside of us. Jesus warns us about this:

> And He [Jesus] said, "What comes out of a man; that defiles a man. For from within, out of the heart of men, proceed evil thoughts, adulteries, fornications, murders, thefts, covetousness, wickedness, deceit, lewdness, an evil eye, blasphemy, pride, foolishness. All these evil things come from within and defile a man." (Mark 7:20–23)

> Judge not, that you be not judged. For with what judgment you judge, you will be judged; and with the measure you use, it will be measured back to you. And why do you look at the speck in your brother's eye, but do not consider the plank in your own eye? Or how can you say to your brother, "Let me remove the speck from your eye"; and look, a plank is in your own eye? Hypocrite! First remove the plank from your own eye, and then you will see clearly to remove the speck from your brother's eye. (Matt. 7:1–5)

We cannot live as if we are exempt from obeying God's Word simply because someone has hurt us. For example, God commands us to love Him with our whole being and to love others as we love ourselves. Nowhere in Scripture are we given permission to be mean, ugly, hateful or indifferent because of another's behavior or attitude. God's grace is sufficient for us in any and every situation, but first we must recognize our sin and repent; only then can we be properly used as God's holy tools for others' redemption and restoration.

The bottom line of this chapter is summed up by Jesus' answer to the Pharisees about which command is the most important: "One of their religion scholars spoke for them, posing a question they hoped would show him up: 'Teacher, which command in God's Law is the most important?' Jesus said, "'Love the Lord your God with all your passion and prayer and intelligence." This is the most important, the first on any list. But there is a second to set alongside it: "Love others as well as you love yourself." These two commands are pegs; everything in God's Law and the Prophets hangs from them'" (Matt. 22:36–40, MSG).

Why do you think Jesus responded this way to these religious leaders? _____
_____
_____
_____

What does it mean to "love the LORD your God with all your heart, with all your soul, and with all your mind" (NKJV)? _____
_____
_____

How does this command challenge you personally? _____
_____
_____
_____

What does it mean to love others as well as you love yourself? _____
_____
_____

Do you think there are exceptions to this command? If so, what are they? _____
_____
_____

In which relationship(s) do you find it most difficult to love the other as yourself? Why? _____
_____
_____

God commands us to love Him with our whole being and to love others as we love ourselves.

We would prefer the Lord to just give us a specific to-do list on how to be the wife of an addict, but, unfortunately, God didn't inspire any writer—Old or New Testament—to write a special chapter for the wives of men trapped in the life-dominating sin of drug abuse and misuse, alcoholism, pornography, gambling, people-pleasing or any other form of bondage in this fallen world. Probably the most difficult thing most of us have done is to try to live in a meaningful relationship with an addict. Living day in and day out with someone who is walking contrary to holiness and godliness—especially when it twists and violates all the rules that make living together in unity possible—simply is not an easy thing to do. Yet *it is possible* when God's Spirit is alive and active in you and when you acknowledge that, apart from the abundant grace of God, all are guilty and without a shred of hope.

Self-righteousness

As the wife of a former addict, I must say that I often thought, felt and believed that I was a righteous woman. After all, *I* didn't do any of the things my husband did. I was the one who was there for our children. I was the one who kept things going when he was messing up. I was faithful and true to him always, never once considering another man. *I was right before God and he was so very wrong*. This was the prevailing attitude of my heart. From this heart I spoke to the Lord God *about* my husband; lots of time passed before I learned to go to God in prayer *for* my husband.

The fact that I don't snort coke, smoke crack, drink, gamble, etc., means *nothing* at the foot of the cross. No one was, is or ever will be good enough to stand worthy before the throne of God without being covered by the atoning blood of Jesus Christ. Some of us may think we are, but the Bible is clear on this: "What then? Are we better than they? Not at all. For we have previously charged both Jews and Greeks that they are all under sin. As it is written: There is none righteous, no, not one" (Rom. 3:9–10).

Any time you are confronted with sin, either in your life or the life of another, remember that the truth of the gospel applies the same to one and all. "This righteousness from God comes through faith in Jesus Christ to all who believe. There is no difference, for *all have sinned and fall short* of the glory of God" (Rom. 3:22–23, NIV).

How does knowing that we are all equal sinners in need of God's mercy, forgiveness and wisdom alter your self-perception? _____

_____

So, if all sin is equal, what do I mean when I talk about "life-dominating sin?" According to the Biblical Counseling Foundation, "When you willingly or unknowingly are under the control of any power other than God's Holy Spirit (ex., drugs, alcohol, sex, another person, your peer group, a false religion, a self-centered habit such as gossip or laziness, or a self-oriented desire for power, food or wealth) you are in bondage to sin."[2] (This sin usually dominates your life.)

As you consider this definition, can you think of any area of your life that you have repeatedly tried to change yet continue to practice? Stretch your thinking beyond just drugs and alcohol. For example, overeating, overspending, anger/bitterness, verbal explosions, etc., can be life-dominating problems. Think about your answer for a moment, then answer the following questions:

How does your response differ from what your husband would answer, and how is it similar? _____

_____

_____

_____

How are you currently doing at surrendering that area to Christ? _____

_____

_____

_____

In our ministry we counsel many women who can't go an hour without a cigarette, or who are so twisted up with anger, bitterness and resentment that their husbands haven't heard them speak a kind word in ages—yet their ability to understand the compelling nature of their husband's addiction escapes them.

I am well-acquainted with this mode of operation, because I've done the same thing. I was not kind or compassionate toward my husband—I was miserable. Every time he lied or did any number of things, I felt my hopes and dreams for a happy life being squashed. So when I was mean, I deceived myself and blamed him. I justified myself by saying something like, "I would never have done that or said that if *he* hadn't . . ." Does that sound familiar?

Addiction so grossly impacts our lives that it can cripple our ability to view ourselves accurately; thus we become convinced that the "little sins" we commit are nothing compared to what our husbands have done. The truth is, however, that if we allow sin to dwell in our bodies, be it an addiction or a harsh and hateful tongue, we deceive ourselves. It is never okay to sin against other people just because they sin against us.

Read Romans 12:9. What do you think false love with hypocrisy looks like? _____
_____

By contrast what do you think sincere love without hypocrisy looks like? _____
_____

How can you show sincere love without hypocrisy to your husband? _____
_____

To others? _____

Unless we wrestle with the huge emotions that stir us and take our souls in hand and make them obedient to the Word of God, we will not do better. Jesus tells us, "'Most assuredly I say to you, whoever commits sin is a slave to sin'" (John 8:34). Just like our husbands must deal with their sin lest they continue to be a slave to it, so must we!

> What shall we say then? Shall we continue in sin that grace may abound? Certainly not! How shall we who died to sin live any longer in it? . . . knowing this, that our old man was crucified with Him, that the body of sin, might be done away with, that we should no longer be slaves of sin. For He who has died has been freed from sin. . . . Likewise you also, reckon yourselves dead indeed to sin, but alive to God in Christ Jesus our Lord. Therefore, do not let sin reign in your mortal bodies, that you should obey it and its lusts. And do not present your members as instruments of unrighteousness to sin, but present yourselves to God as being alive from the dead, and your members as instruments of righteousness to God. (Rom. 6:1–2, 6–7, 11–13)

Are you knowingly sinning in any area of your life? How might you be justifying your behaviors and attitudes? Be specific. _____
_____
_____
_____
_____

Ask God to show you any behaviors and attitudes that you believe exist because of other people in your life. What might they be? _____

_____

_____

"If we say we have no sin, we deceive ourselves, and the truth is not in us. If we confess our sins, He is faithful and just to forgive us our sins and to cleanse us from all unrighteousness. If we say we have not sinned, we make Him a liar, and His word is not in us" (1 John 1:8–10).

Read John 3:19–21. What things do you prefer to keep hidden? _____

_____

God calls you to acknowledge, confess and repent of your sinful attitudes and behaviors. What is the Lord leading you to confess? _____

_____

What does He promise to do? _____

_____

Second Timothy 2:22 says, "Flee also youthful lusts; but pursue righteousness, faith, love, peace with those who call on the Lord out of a pure heart." So what exactly do righteousness, faith, love and peace look like? I've defined a few of the terms from this verse to help you use Scripture, rather than your husband, as your standard of comparison.

Righteous: morally upright; without guilt or sin
Faith: belief that does not rest on logical proof or material evidence
Love: read First Corinthians 13 (it's all in there)
Peace: freedom from quarrels and disagreements

I fell way short of correct living, according to the words of Second Timothy 2:22, because I didn't call on the Lord from a pure heart. More often than not, my life looked righteous to me because, compared to my husband, I was living a good Christian life. I think it's safe to say, however, that was my view but not God's.

Be honest with yourself with Jesus as your standard of comparison. How do you compare according to His righteousness? His love? His peace? _____

_____

_____

Taking the time to consider Timothy's words helps us see things from a proper, biblical perspective. I hope you're beginning to see a bigger picture—one not based on how you feel but rather on who God is and who we are because of Him.

Read First Peter 4:1–11 and you will see that:

✧ Christ suffered and died to destroy sin.

✧ you are not alone in your suffering.

- ✧ Christ never gave in to the least little sin.
- ✧ as tempted as you may be to strike back, you can be ruled by the Spirit resisting the temptation to be ruled by your own passions.

Christ gives you the power to resist sin, and He will transform your heart, which will result in a change in the way you think, the way you judge and the way you feel and act. Remember your conversion experience; repent of any and all wrong-doing; embrace God's grace and power to transform you.

As you mature in your faith, it will become less natural for you to do the things you did in the past. You will allow Christ in you to govern your responses, especially those to your husband. You will be pleasantly surprised when you don't give in to your normal reactions and allow others to push your buttons.

I used to allow my anger to get so big that I'd withhold my affection and my acts of service to my husband. For instance, sometimes I didn't greet him in love or didn't prepare dinner for him with the same care. In my spirit there would be much grumbling and complaining. Nothing I did for him was seasoned with grace, but it definitely should have been.

Read First Corinthians 15:33. How are you influenced by others' poor attitudes and behaviors? _____
_____
_____

Sometimes we have to remain faithful through difficult situations; how can you maintain your good character in a less-than-perfect environment? _____
_____

First Peter 4:7–11 gives us some encouragement:

> The end of all things is at hand; therefore be self-controlled and sober-minded for the sake of your prayers. Above all, *keep loving one another earnestly, since love covers a multitude of sins.* Show hospitality to one another without grumbling. As each has received a gift, use it to serve one another, as good stewards of God's varied grace: whoever speaks, as one who speaks oracles of God; whoever serves, as one who serves by the strength that God supplies—in order that in everything God may be glorified through Jesus Christ. To him belong glory and dominion forever and ever. Amen. (ESV)

Take the time now to pause and pray this simple prayer, as David did in Psalm 139:23–24:

> Search me, O God, and know my heart;
> try me and know my anxieties;
> And see if there is any wicked way in me,
> And lead me in the way everlasting!

I encourage you to inspect your own heart through the lens of Scripture on a regular basis to see if there "is any wicked way in you."

As you read these Scriptures, question how they relate it to your present life and how they challenge you or call you to interact with your spouse.

Psalm 32:1–5. Do you feel the Lord's hand is heavy upon you? _____
_____

In what ways?_____

_____

What steps do you have to take to be forgiven? _____

When you confess your sin, how do you feel differently about it? _____

_____

Proverbs 16:16–19. In what ways do you struggle with pride (which can be very subtle) in your life?
_____

How do you respond differently when someone who has sinned against you comes with a humble spirit rather than a proud spirit? _____

How does knowing that *all* deeds will be exposed make you feel? _____

_____

Ephesians 4:1–3. How does this Scripture impress you relative to your present life situation? _____

_____

_____

What one change can you implement immediately in response to this verse? _____

_____

Ephesians 5:11. Are there ways you are participating in the unfruitful ways of others? _____

_____

_____

What have you done to expose unfruitful ways of darkness? In yourself? _____

_____

In others? _____

_____

Hebrews 12:14. Have you done all that is up to you to live at peace with others in your life? _____

_____

If not, what else can you do to live at peace with others? _____

_____

_____

James 1:22–25. Are you obedient to what you know is true in God's Word? _____

When you are challenged by a sermon, a Scripture or a comment from a loving friend, what is you typical response? _____

James 5:16. A huge component of correct living is being in Christian fellowship—attending regular services and having an accountability partner. Who is a Christian sister you know who could come alongside you so you can confess to and pray for one another? _____

Will you ask her to join you on this journey? _____

First Peter 2:1–3. Evil only breeds more evil. Do you see any malice, hypocrisy, envy or evil speaking in your own life? _____ In what way? _____
_____

How will you cast them off? _____
_____

What do you have to overcome to steep yourself in the truth of the Word? _____
_____

Taking journeys through Scripture like these are vital to knowing how to biblically respond to life's situations. For us to understand how to respond to a person struggling with sin, it is critical that we examine our own life before the Lord. In order to do that, we must know and understand God's Word as it pertains to our own hearts and minds.

The point is that it's not our opinion that matters; it is the truth of God's Word that matters. If I am not living according to God's truth, how can I ever speak truth, peppered with grace and mercy, into someone else's life? My actions will always speak louder than my words.

Let me ask you: Do you see yourself as blameless? Would others see you as blameless? Are there any areas of your life that your husband or children could point to as not being quite level with the Bible's teachings? _____
_____
_____

Sometimes you may not be doing anything biblically *wrong*, yet you may be causing another to stumble. For example, in my years of counseling ministry, it has been necessary, on occasion, to strongly encourage a wife not to drink. "All things are lawful for me, but not all things are helpful; all things are lawful for me, but not all things edify. Let no one seek his own, but each one the other's well-being" (1 Cor. 10:23–24). You see, *for her* drinking is not a sin. It simply doesn't grip her by the throat as it does her loved one, so she has the liberty to drink without sinning. What she is challenged to consider is the fact that *for him*, it is sin, so by drinking, she sets a stumbling block before him. "Therefore let us not judge one another anymore, but rather resolve this, not to put a stumbling block or a cause to fall in our brother's way" (Rom. 14:1). In essence she is sinning against her "weaker brother." We are called by God to love our brother. We are also given freedom in Christ, but the law of love supersedes the law of liberty. In other words, we forgo our freedom for the sake of love.

In what ways do you intentionally or unintentionally place a stumbling block before your husband?
_____
_____

We must never forget that sin is sin is sin, and no matter who does the sinning, sin is not okay with God. Erase any lines you have drawn to separate your actions or sins from your husband's. Choose today to be on God's side, to see things as He sees them, seeking to do all that is up to you to do to live at peace with your husband and others. "Let your light so shine before men, that they may see your good works and glorify your Father in heaven" (Matt. 5:16). "For you were bought at a price; therefore glorify God in your body and in your spirit, which are God's. Therefore, whether you eat or drink, or whatever you do, do all to the glory of God" (1 Cor. 6:20; 10:31).

Application

You may be wondering how to assimilate this information and put it to proactive use in your life. Before you give in to the temptation to be overwhelmed, let me encourage you by saying that the sole purpose for the above section is to give you a solid, foundational understanding of scriptural facts. As you interact with your husband concerning a particular area of sin, you will see how some of the above plays out in your life, and you will have a storehouse of truth to apply to the situation. Hosea 4:6 says, "My people are destroyed for lack of knowledge." Grab hold of the truth of God's Word and hold fast to it. Your very life depends on it!

What does it mean to you to grab hold of the truth of God's Word? _____
_____

How do you/can you hold fast to truth? _____
_____

Living life as a true follower of Jesus Christ is hugely impacted and governed by the gospel and the truth of the Word. Paul's words to the church of Philippi are challenging and encouraging:

> Only let your conduct be worthy of the gospel of Christ, so that whether I come and see you or am absent, I may hear of your affairs, that you stand fast in one spirit, with one mind striving together for the faith of the gospel, and not in any way terrified by your adversaries, which is to them a proof of perdition [loss of the soul; eternal damnation], but to you of salvation, and that from God. For to you it has been granted on behalf of Christ, not only to believe in Him, but also to suffer for His sake, having the same conflict which you saw in me and now hear is in me. (Phil. 1:27–30)

It isn't difficult to serve our husbands *as long as everything goes our way*, according to the plan that we have consciously or unconsciously written on our hearts since we were little girls. But here we are, having made choices, some good and some bad, and we've discovered that life refuses to be tied up in a neat little package. Life happens, and it does so without our permission or control. We therefore need to be ready to make a conscious choice to reflect Christ.

So now that we have a clearer understanding of what life-dominating sin is, let's consider how to set our sights on what is truly important.

Focus on God First

We need to get our focus off others in our lives who are hurting us and focus on the Almighty One who has the power and ability to bring change. We are great at looking for a change of heart—and hopefully a change of mind—in our husband. We know exactly how we want him to be—*if only he would see it.* Yet God has often said to me, "You know, Stephanie, I really don't want him to do it your way or see it your way. *My ways* are higher, and *My ways* are best." You see, God wants our hearts. He woos and pursues us for the purpose of drawing us ever closer to Himself. His desire is that we lay our wants at His feet and say, with a surrendered heart, "Not my will, but Yours, be done" (Luke 22:42). More often than not, these words are prayed through travailing tears. I don't know anyone who has ever said these words with a smile on her face. Jesus Himself shed tears from the agony and anguish He bore in His soul in the Garden of Gethsemane as, knowing what lay ahead for Him at Golgotha, He bowed before His Father.

I know what it feels like to have your heart bruised by addiction. As the wife of a former addict, my eyes have wept many tears. I wish I could say that I cried as many tears for my husband as I did for myself, but I can't. I spent more time crying because *I* was hurt and wounded than I did because I was concerned for *him*. I share this to encourage you not to do the same. Sure, cry for yourself. Tell God all about your anger, bitterness and resentment. Allow Him to hear your heart in all its misery. Just don't get stuck there! Stay on your knees before Him in confession and repentance. Receive cleansing and healing from Him—and new strength to start believing afresh that He is able to do in you and through you a new and better thing.

Refuse to be a casualty of war! Refuse to give up and to give in to the lie that you are without hope or help. God sees you! God hears you! God knows you! The Sovereign God is aware of you. Don't hide any part of yourself for fear of how you will sound or look to Him. If there is anyone you can be real with, it is Him. Is it possible to live like we truly believe God is watching?

> O Lord, You have searched me and known me.
> You know my sitting down and my rising up;
>> You understand my thought afar off.
> You comprehend my path and my lying down,
>> And are acquainted with all my ways.
> For there is not a word on my tongue,
>> But behold, O Lord, You know it altogether.
> You have hedged me behind and before,
>> And laid Your hand upon me.
> Such knowledge is too wonderful for me;
>> It is high, I cannot attain it. (Ps. 139:1–6)

Do you live in constant awareness that God sees you? _____

How does that impact you? _____

> Where can I go from Your Spirit?
>> Or where can I flee from Your presence?
> If I ascend into heaven, You are there;
>> If I make my bed in hell, behold, You are there.
> If I take the wings of the morning,
>> And dwell in the uttermost parts of the sea,
> Even there Your hand shall lead me,

And Your right hand shall hold me.
If I say, "Surely the darkness shall fall on me,"
   Even the night shall be light about me;
Indeed, the darkness shall not hide from You,
   But the night shines as the day;
   The darkness and the light are both alike to You. (139:7–12)

When you want to flee, where (or how) do you hide? _____

How does knowing God is there for you comfort your soul? _____
_____
_____

For You formed my inward parts;
   You covered me in my mother's womb.
I will praise You, for I am fearfully and wonderfully made;
   Marvelous are Your works,
   And that my soul knows very well.
My frame was not hidden from You,
   When I was made in secret,
   And skillfully wrought in the lowest parts of the earth.
Your eyes saw my substance, being yet unformed.
   And in Your book they all were written,
   The days fashioned for me,
   When as yet there were none of them.

How precious also are Your thoughts to me, O God!
   How great is the sum of them!
If I should count them, they would be more in number than the sand;
   When I awake, I am still with You. . . .

Search me, O God, and know my heart;
   Try me, and know my anxieties;
And see if there is any wicked way in me,
   And lead me in the way everlasting. (139:13–18, 23–24)

Focus on Yourself Second

By focusing on God first rather than yourself, it should be virtually impossible to stand in a place of self-righteous condemnation of your husband—even if he relapses into his former sin pattern—because you will see your own standing before God. You will be better equipped to intercede on his behalf in prayer and to make humble choices that are necessary to create an environment that will make it difficult for this sin to continue and abound.

Remember, you are a strong woman in the Lord, and God has equipped you with everything you need to handle your situation in the present. Understand that when I say you're a strong woman, I'm saying it's okay that you are strong. As P.B. Wilson writes, "God has no problem with you being a strong woman. He loves strong women."[3]

I have been strong and outspoken most of my life. More often than not, in times of conflict, I have exercised this strength in a rebellious way. I've justified my expressions of strength—both because I was in pain and wanted out of it and because fighting back came naturally to me.

Have you used your strong temperament sinfully in relationship to your husband? How so? _____
_____
_____
_____

God is not caught by surprise when we don't respond biblically. The Lord wants us to see our true selves and to submit our whole heart, soul, mind and strength to Him. He wants us to bring our strength to the table, but then we need to lay it there for Him to mold and shape according to the wisdom of His Word. He wants us to surrender our strength, our own "wisdom" and our flawed ways of trying to bring Him glory.

Choose today, dear sister, to take back any ground the Enemy has stolen from you and to say no to what you perceive to be your right to scream, yell, shut down, withhold love, give dirty looks, talk down, nag, whine, complain, use bad language, gossip, slander, etc. Those of us who have done things from this list know the real truth (not the truth we convince ourselves to believe)—it's all a waste of time. Bickering and fighting doesn't get you anywhere. Philippians exhorts, "Do all things without complaining and disputing, that you may become blameless and harmless, children of God without fault in the midst of a crooked and perverse generation, among whom shine as lights in the world, holding fast the word of life, so that I may rejoice in the day of Christ that I have not run in vain or labored in vain" (2:14–16).

I remember the day God begin to show me my true self. For years I had justified my rebellious attitude toward my husband. In my heart I believed that I would be less contentious and rebellious if he would be the man he was called to be. As long as he was messing up, I didn't think it was necessary or even possible for me to surrender control. I murmured, complained and argued—sincerely hoping it would make a difference. It sounds crazy when I think about it. It was quite a blow to my ego and pride when the impact of God's Word on my heart and mind brought me to tears. But, you see, when our ways and our thoughts are separated from God's ways and thoughts, our perspective is warped, and we act, think and live wrongly.

Have you ever seen yourself (or do you see yourself now) willing to sin to get your way—thinking *if he wasn't doing "a," I wouldn't have to do "b."* Share some examples: _____
_____
_____
_____
_____

As I said, I remember the day the truth hit me. I was in my car listening to the radio, and Bunny Wilson was speaking about the "s word." You know the one I mean—submission. She quoted First Samuel 15:23: "For rebellion is as the sin of witchcraft, and stubbornness is as iniquity and idolatry." I asked myself, how is rebellion like witchcraft? Bunny went on to explain:

> Witchcraft is designed to make a person do what you want them to do. The Lord says when you murmur and complain, when you pout and you nag and you give the silent treatment, He said it's just like practicing witchcraft, because what you're saying to your husband is, "I will go back to being the wonderful person you always knew if you do things the way I want them done."[4]

When I heard this, I was devastated. The very thought that God would equate anything I could do to witchcraft and idolatry was offensive to my spirit. Even though I could self-righteously justify everything I did, I knew and God knew that I had sinned against my husband. It didn't matter if my husband was in the middle of his addiction or not—I was to submit to God and deny myself the right to do a whole slew of things I had thus far allowed myself.

Bunny continued:

> He [God] said that my rebellion (rebellion against Him and His way) is like practicing witchcraft, and stubbornness is like idolatry, because idolatry is when we worship something above God. It could be your ministry, it could be your children, your money, your profession—it could be a lot of things that you worship above God that's idolatry; but He says when you are stubborn against My established order in your home, in your job, in your church, He said you are worshipping your thoughts, your feelings, and your opinions above what My Word teaches and as far as I'm concerned that is like practicing idolatry.
>
> Now, I don't know about you, but when God calls an angel over and says, "That's Bunny— she's my child," I don't want any adjectives like rebellious, stubborn, contentious, argumentative, deceitful, manipulative or guileful before my name. I want to be God's yielded, submitted servant. I want to be kind, compassionate, empathetic, sympathetic, willing and obedient.[5]

Like Bunny, I decided to let go of my rebelliousness, and it has been good, good, good! Note that I did not say that it has been easy. Far from it! But God is faithful to do that which He has promised when we submit our wills to His.

You too must decide to surrender to the Lord. I encourage you to decide, first and foremost, to wholly serve Him. Meditate on Second Chronicles 7:14: "If My people who are called by My name will humble themselves, and pray and seek My face, and turn from their wicked ways, then I will hear from heaven, and will forgive their sin and heal their land." Pause to ask God what He desires you to repent of. Then repent, or "feel such regret for past conduct as to change one's mind regarding it,"[6] and renounce your sin, refusing to recognize or obey it any longer.

The Lord will give you the necessary power to overcome every struggle; He will equip you with the necessary tools for victory. "For the weapons of our warfare are not carnal but mighty in God for pulling down strongholds, casting down arguments and every high thing that exalts itself against the knowledge of God, bringing every thought into captivity to the obedience of Christ" (2 Cor. 10:4–5).

Write out your thoughts and your prayer: _____

_____

_____

_____

_____

_____

I'm hoping you are beginning to get a hint of what is possible in your relationship with your husband when God has first place in all that you think, say and do. Don't just walk around *pretending* to believe the truth that is expressed here, walking around in abject denial while professing, "Just give it all to the Lord." Sisters, friends—believe God! Believe God is all that He says He is whether or not you can imagine, think or see it. Are you feeling controlled by defeat, anger, frustration or unbelief? Are you afraid to trust God with all your hopes and dreams? If God says He is your Deliverer, then you can trust Him to deliver you from whatever has you bound. So will you be the conqueror in Christ Jesus that God says you are and overcome by force the grip that unbelief has on your heart and mind? Will you praise God no matter what? Will you look the Enemy in the face, and with all your armor on, say to him that he cannot have any of the territory that is yours, and as long as you are on watch here, he shall not pass! Stand your ground!

Read Ephesians 6:10–18, and list the pieces of the armor of God:

1. _____
2. _____
3. _____
4. _____
5. _____
6. _____

We need to be "dressed" properly if we are to stand firm. We need to remember the saving power of the gospel and its protective armor.

According to Ephesians, why should you put on the armor of God?

1. _____
2. _____

What do we battle against? _____

When and how are we to pray? _____

I'm including a paraphrase of Ephesians 6:13–18 from *The Message* for your personal edification. As you read it, allow the Holy Spirit to speak boldness into your heart and a fire into your bones to equip you to stay the course and finish well.

> And that about wraps it up. God is strong, and he wants you strong. So take everything the Master has set out for you, well-made weapons of the best materials. And put them to use so you will be able to stand up to everything the Devil throws your way. This is no afternoon athletic contest that we'll walk away from and forget about in a couple of hours. This is for keeps, a life-or-death fight to the finish

against the Devil and all his angels. Be prepared. You're up against far more than you can handle on your own. Take all the help you can get, every weapon God has issued, so that when it's all over but the shouting you'll still be on your feet. Truth, righteousness, peace, faith, and salvation are more than words. Learn how to apply them. You'll need them throughout your life. God's Word is an indispensable weapon. In the same way, prayer is essential in this ongoing warfare. Pray hard and long. Pray for your brothers and sisters. Keep your eyes open. Keep each other's spirits up so that no one falls behind or drops out.

It would be wonderful not to bear the burden of being on watch over my family and my husband in prayer and fasting. I know I would gladly give over the weight of that particular duty. But if this is what is to be, then so be it. I will stand watch until I draw my last breath.

Yet there is victory to be had here on earth. Through many trials my husband has come to a place of believing that he is who God says he is. He believes that—one day at a time—he can and will walk in the victory that is his in Christ Jesus—not just victory over drinking and drugs but victory over lies and the father of all lies.

Dear sisters, as I bring this chapter to a close, I leave you with the following thoughts for you to pause and ponder:

✦ Resist the temptation to "go it alone," thus forsaking the ministry of the body of Christ.
 • Stay in fellowship with your church, and allow someone to get close enough to you to speak the truth to you and hold you accountable.

✦ Don't allow your life to revolve around the addiction.
 • Maintain as much order in your life and the lives of your kids as possible.

✦ Remember that you too are a person in need of change.
 • Refuse to let self-righteous pride get the best of you.

✦ Keep growing.
 • During difficult times it is easy to get so caught up in the trials and stresses of our situation that we allow our time alone with God, our attendance at Sunday worship, our participation in Bible study, etc., to slowly diminish. Then voilà! We stop growing, and we may even find ourselves slipping into our old sinful habits.

✦ Stay in the present.
 • Choose to keep your thoughts from running ahead of you. Much of our reaction and stress is related to fear of what tomorrow will bring. Live life in the present, and receive God's grace for each moment. You can't borrow grace for tomorrow when it isn't your reality yet. Make decisions only as they arise for each day.

✦ Do not keep score.
 • In other words, keep no record of wrongs. The ground is level at the foot of the cross, and we must resist the temptation to keep track of the other person's wrongs.

✦ Throw away your eraser.
 • Let's say your husband has walked free from substance abuse for six months, and for whatever

reason (which you may never understand), he relapses for a day or two. You're crushed. How could he do it? How could he relapse when he was doing so well? You lament, cry and moan over the injustice of it all. It feels like you're all the way back at square one, and he needs to start all over again to prove himself worthy of your trust and respect. In other words, you erase the six good months and act like they never happened. Yet God's Word calls us to choose grace and mercy. You do not want to be a stumbling block; you want to be a strong voice of encouragement and hope.

✦ Avoid playing Sherlock Holmes.
  • I don't know about you, but the more I investigated into my husband's life, the more I needed to. I felt like I *had* to know what was going on. Thinking about what he was doing all the time consumed more energy than I had to spare, and it wreaked havoc on my body. You don't have to be the one to regulate and control his comings and goings and all he does in between. When you find yourself in the middle of some such activity, stop and reflect: what is going on in your head? Where is God in your situation?

✦ Remember that forgiveness is always a choice before it becomes a feeling.
  • "Be kind to one another, tenderhearted, forgiving one another, even as God in Christ forgave you" (Eph. 4:32).

✦ Develop patience.
  • "To receive the harvest and the crown of life that you deserve, you must persevere. The testing of faith produces patience (the ability to endure). Only under trial can the believer test the true depth of his faith in God. The established heart will not waiver, but will rejoice in the knowledge of the goodness of God."[7]

✦ Sing and give glory to God. Cry out to Him.
  • "But I will sing of Your power; Yes, I will sing aloud of Your mercy in the morning. For You have been my defense and refuge in the day of my trouble. To You, O my Strength, I will sing praises, for God is my defense, my God of mercy" (Ps. 59:16–17).

  • "Because Your loving-kindness is better than life, my lips shall praise You" (Ps. 63:3).

  • "Rejoice the soul of Your servant. For to You, O LORD, I lift up my soul. For You, Lord, are good and ready to forgive, and abundant in mercy to all who call upon You. Give ear O LORD to my prayer, and attend to the voice of my supplications" (Ps. 86:4–6).

✦ Be hungry for the God of the Bible.
  • At one time you ate, drank, slept, lived and breathed addiction, not of your own but of another. Take a step back. Pick up the living Word that is inhabited by the breath of God, and eat it, drink it, sleep it and breathe it as if your life depends on it—because it does!

✦ Be who you are.
  • Avoid the temptation to walk on egg shells, living in fear that what you do might *cause* your husband to stumble and fall back into his addiction. He will do what he will do. You must simply do what is up to you to do and leave the rest to the Lord. It is not your responsibility to change him or keep him clean, drug and alcohol free.

Sisters, choose to believe. Choose grace. Choose to hope. *There is hope.* Remember in the midst of it all, you are protected by the Father, through Jesus the Son, and empowered by the Holy Spirit!

"May the God of hope fill you with all joy and peace as you trust in him, so that you may overflow with hope by the power of the Holy Spirit" (Rom. 15:13, NIV).

Application Questions

1. What one or two statements impacted me from this chapter?

   a. _____

   b. _____

2. How can I apply it/them to my life today and begin to pursue positive growth? _____
   _____

3. What one step am I willing to take to move toward heart change in my reactions, behavior or attitude? _____
   _____

4. What do I learn about God from this chapter? _____
   _____

5. How does His Word (the Bible) confirm this? _____
   _____
   _____

6

Instruments of Righteousness: Our Words, God's Purposes

by Diane Hunt

But rather offer yourselves to God, as those who have been brought from death to life; and offer the parts of your body to Him as instruments of righteousness.

Romans 6:13

This is not a typical Bible study on communication. In fact, our focus will be more on the issues of your heart than on communication skills. I would venture to guess that you know how to communicate but either can't, won't or don't do it. The how-to's are not the problem; the problem is the motives of our hearts, which show through our words. "For out of the abundance of the heart the mouth speaks" (Matt. 12:34).

Our words are a powerful tool for good, or ill. We can empower others to strive and reach their potential, or we can tear them down or hold them back. With our words we can bring out either the best or the worst in others. Your words even have a powerful effect on you. "A man's stomach shall be satisfied from the fruit of his mouth; from the produce of his lips he shall be filled" (Prov. 18:20). Like any attribute with the power of the Holy Spirit, our words can be a fantastic asset; or, in the power of our own flesh, we can use them to hurt and emaciate. I love what Beth Moore says: "God's words are omnipotent, and since we are made in His image, our words are potent."[1]

Write Proverbs 18:21: _____
_____
_____

If we speak negatively, we'll end up eating our words, and this action will affect us as well as our hearers. If we speak positively, we powerfully benefit ourselves as well as our hearers. Our tongues have a great power to heal or to harm:

> Even so the tongue is a little member and boasts great things. See how great a forest a little fire kindles! And the tongue is a fire, a world of iniquity. The tongue is so set among our members that it defiles the whole body, and sets on fire the course of nature; and it is set on fire by hell . . . no man can tame the tongue. It is an unruly evil, full of deadly poison. With it we bless our God and Father, and with it we curse men, who have been made in the similitude of God. Out of the same mouth proceed blessing and cursing. My brethren, these things ought not to be so. (James 3:5–10)

Apart from God's grace and the power of the Holy Spirit, our tongue can do great harm. However, Paul tells us that it has potential for good. Write Ephesians 4:29: _____
_____
_____

What is the purpose for our words? What are we trying to accomplish? Whose agenda are we fulfilling?
_____
_____

Walking in the Spirit requires that we purpose in our hearts to use our words for God's purposes and not our own. "And do not present your members as instruments of unrighteousness to sin, but present yourselves to God as being alive from the dead, and your members as instruments of righteousness to God" (Rom. 6:13).

As we relate this verse to our mouth-member, it is eye-opening to realize that we have only two options; every word we speak is either an instrument of righteousness for God's purposes or an instrument of unrighteousness for Satan's purposes. There is no middle ground.

How do you most often use your mouth-member (other than to eat)? _____
_____

What usually motivates your words? _____

It is not a simple matter of just "keeping our mouths shut." Matthew 12:34 expressly says it is more a heart issue than it is a mouth issue. What comes out of our mouths is a reflection of the issues of our heart. We have all said, "I'm sorry, I didn't mean that!" Guess what? Yes, we did, because our hearts spoke it. Therefore, holding our tongues is not sufficient, because the thought and heart issues still remain. What we need is a new heart attitude.

Instruments of Unrighteousness: Sinful Speech Patterns

Let's look at some ways we use our speech in unrighteous ways, which causes us to accomplish Satan's purposes.

Silence

Pouting, withdrawing, the cold shoulder, avoiding eye contact, the act of "silent murder" (I'll act as if you do not exist).

Can you remember the last time you responded this way in a conflict? What was it about? Why did you go silent? _____
_____
_____
_____

Sarcasm

"Sarcasm" literally means "to tear flesh." It's defined as, "A sharp and often satirical or ironic utterance designed to cut or give pain."[2]

Read Proverbs 12:18. Can you remember a time when someone's sarcasm hurt you? What did the person say? _____

How did it make you feel? _____
_____
_____

Gossip

Gossip involves sharing information that has the potential to damage someone's reputation with someone who is neither part of the problem nor the solution.

Read Proverbs 26:20. Can you think of subtle forms of gossip that you tend to fall prey to? What would they be? _____

_____

_____

How do you balance keeping things to yourself to avoid gossiping (not clamming up and isolating yourself) with sharing information about your husband and/or his addiction with others? _____

_____

_____

_____

_____

Nagging

"To find fault incessantly: a persistent source of annoyance or distraction; to irritate by constant scolding or urging."[3]

Proverbs 27:15–16 tells us, "A continual dripping on a very rainy day and a contentious woman are alike; whoever restrains her restrains the wind, and grasps oil with his right hand."

Although this sinful speech pattern is traditionally associated with the female gender, males are by no means exempt.

If you nag, who are you most likely to nag? About what? _____

_____

_____

_____

If you are not the nagger but the one being nagged, what is the other person usually nagging you about?

_____

_____

_____

Deception

Before you skip over this point, consider that deception comes in many forms. It can be an outright untruth—or it may be a shade of the truth, leaving out some details to intentionally mislead. We may avoid saying something to "keep the peace" or to "avoid his wrath."

Read Ephesians 4:25.

In what ways have you deceived your husband (because of his addiction)? _____

_____

_____

_____

Idle Words or Coarse Jesting

"But I say to you that for every idle word men may speak, they will give account of it in the day of judgment. For by your words you will be justified, and by your words you will be condemned" (Matt. 12:36–37).

We need to guard our words. "And all uncleanness or covetousness, let it not even be named among you, as is fitting for saints; neither filthiness, nor foolish talking, nor coarse jesting, which are not fitting, but rather giving of thanks" (Eph. 5:3–4).

Making Our Point

What is it that makes us think that what we have to say is so vital? We often won't let a conversation rest until we have had our say and feel we have been understood. Yet often in "making our point," we simply say the same thing in a variety of ways. Have you ever found yourself saying the same thing over and over, believing your husband must not understand you yet, because if he did, he would obviously agree with you? It is one thing to have a voice and to share your heart with your husband, but there are times when what pops into your head needs to stay there.

Psalm 12:3–4 says, "May the LORD cut off all flattering lips, And the tongue that speaks proud things, Who have said, 'With our tongue we will prevail; Our lips are our own; Who is lord over us?'" As you look at that Scripture, what are your thoughts? Does it describe you in any way? _____

_____

_____

_____

Cross-Speaking

This is a word I made up to describe speaking to one person while trying to make a point to another person within earshot. My kids have caught me doing this and said, "You weren't even talking to us when you said that!" They were right! My husband was my intended "target."

Telling It "Like It Is"

"I'm just telling the truth like it is." I believe the root of this is pride, going back again to Psalm 12:3–4. There is a variety of ways that we "just speak our minds." The Bible tells us we are to be "speaking the truth in love" (Eph. 4:15) Do you know that speaking the truth without love ceases to be truth because it is tainted by a sinful heart? "Telling it like it is" is only truth *as you see it*. Just speaking our mind can be sin. We hide behind the idea that "it's just the way I am," but that is just a cop out. God is in the process of growing believers in the image of Jesus Christ. Our sinful speech patterns are in the process of being transformed for His glory. "But we all, with unveiled face, beholding as in a mirror the glory of the Lord, are being transformed into the same image from glory to glory, just as by the Spirit of the Lord" (2 Cor. 3:18).

Humor

Humor, rightly used, is a wonderful gift of God created by Him for our pleasure (and probably His). However, misused it can be wielded like a dagger. The old adage, "Many a truth is spoken in jest" is very true. Often our humor can be hurtful, cutting and disrespectful. Our words need to be guided by Ephesians 4:29: "Do not let any unwholesome talk come out of your mouths, but only what is helpful for building others up according to their needs, that it may benefit those who listen" (NIV).

Grumbling and Complaining

Grumbling and complaining are outward evidence of a discontented spirit.

Who do you most often complain to? _____

What do you most often complain about? _____

Who is your complaining against? (Ultimately your complaining is against God since He is over your situation, but there's likely a more obvious earthly target.) _____

_____

Read Philippians 2:14–15. What does it say we will become if we do not grumble and complain? _____

_____

_____

"Now godliness with contentment is great gain" (1 Tim. 6:6).

Criticism or Critical Judgment

A critical person is "inclined to criticize severely and unfavorably"[4] and tends to find fault with others.

As you look over this list, determine which of these sinful speech patterns you struggle with most. Why do you think it is specifically a problem for you? _____

_____

_____

Let's consider some ways God can use our mouths to accomplish His purposes.

Instruments of Righteousness: A Godly Use of Words

Often our greatest concern about our speech is the detrimental effect it has on our relationships, but we should have a greater concern—it grieves the heart of God. We need to remember we live *coram Deo*, before the face of God.

Putting off sinful speech is not enough. Whenever we are called to put off a sinful pattern, we are always called to put on a holy pattern. "But you have not so learned Christ, if indeed you have heard Him and have been taught by Him, as the truth is in Jesus: that you put off, concerning your former conduct, the old man which grows corrupt according to the deceitful lusts, and be renewed in the spirit of your mind, and that you put on the new man which was created according to God, in true righteousness and holiness" (Eph. 4:20–24). So what are some biblical ways to use words? _____

_____

_____

_____

Speak Truth

Ephesians 4:15 commands us to be a part of Christ's body that "speaks the truth in love," and this concept is most aptly applied to speaking the truth of God's Word into another's life and heart. God's Word, especially when spoken in love, is a powerful tool. Read Psalm 119 as it is full of verses regarding the power, value and beauty of God's Word.

Encourage

"To inspire with courage, spirit, or hope, hearten; to spur on, stimulate; to give help or patronage to; foster."[5]

Read how in Acts 15:30–32 Paul encourages the believers in Antioch.

When was the last time someone encouraged you, and what did that person do or say? _____

_____

_____

_____

When was the last time you encouraged someone, and what did you do or say? _____
_____
_____

Look for positive things about a person and intentionally point them out. When you pray for someone, drop a note or mention to the person that you brought him/her before the throne of grace.

Edify

"Build; establish; to instruct or improve especially in moral and religious knowledge."[6] "Therefore comfort each other and edify one another, just as you also are doing" (1 Thess. 5:11).

I know it is difficult to want to edify someone who has hurt you, but what are a couple ways you could build that person up? _____
_____

Bless

"To invoke divine care for; to speak well of; to confer prosperity or happiness upon."[7]

Romans 12:14 tells us, "Bless those who persecute you; bless and do not curse." How much more should we bless those we love!

"Finally, all of you be of one mind, having compassion for one another; love as brothers, be tender-hearted, be courteous; not returning evil for evil or reviling for reviling, but on the contrary blessing, knowing that you were called to this, that you may inherit a blessing" (1 Pet. 3:8–9).

Instruct

"To give knowledge to: teach, train; to provide with authoritative information or advice; to give an order or command to direct."[8]

Read Proverbs 16:21. What does it say increases learning? _____
What do you think that looks like? _____
_____
_____

Exhort

"To incite by argument or advice; make urgent appeals."[9]

"Exhort one another daily, while it is called 'Today', lest any of you be hardened through the deceitfulness of sin" (Heb. 3:13).

Exhortation means humbly applying God's Word to one's circumstances; keep Him at the center!

Admonish

"To indicate duties or obligations to; to express warning or disapproval to especially in a gentle, earnest, or solicitous manner; to give friendly earnest advice or encouragement to."[10]

"Let the word of Christ dwell in you richly in all wisdom, teaching and admonishing one another in psalms and hymns and spiritual songs, singing with grace in your hearts to the Lord" (Col. 3:16).

Rebuke

Reprimand: a severe or formal reproof; correction.[11]

"Like an earring of gold and an ornament of fine gold is a wise rebuker to an obedient ear" (Prov. 25:12).

Comfort

"To give strength and hope, to cheer; to ease the grief or trouble of, console."[12]

Write Proverbs 12:25: _____

_____

Can you identify with anxious depression? How? _____

_____

_____

What "good word" might have encouraged you at that time? _____

_____

Implementing Truth: Applying What You Have Learned

Repent

When we realize that we have been disobeying or offending God with our tongue, we must repent. Turn away from sin and turn toward God.

As you scan through the unrighteous manners of speech above, in what areas do you sense God's Spirit convicting you to repent? _____

_____

Write out your prayer of repentance to God: _____

_____

_____

_____

_____

Remember, as First John 1:9 tells us, "If we confess our sins, He is faithful and just to forgive us our sins and to cleanse us from all unrighteousness."

Pray

Acknowledge your need for God's help. You will not gain victory apart from the Holy Spirit.

"If any of you lacks wisdom, let him ask of God, who gives to all liberally and without reproach, and it will be given to him" (James 1:5).

Commit Your Mouth to God

Before getting out of bed every morning, ask the Lord to be your mouth's guardian.

"Set a guard, O LORD, over my mouth; Keep watch over the door of my lips" (Ps. 141:3).

Ask God to accomplish His purposes through you, through your mouth today. "And do not present your members as instruments of unrighteousness to sin, but present yourselves to God as being alive from the dead, and your members as instruments of righteousness to God" (Rom. 6:13). Remember, every time you open your mouth, you are either an instrument of Satan, for his purposes, or God, for His purposes. In whose camp do you want to pitch your tent?

Pray that you might, like the psalmist, be able to say to the Lord, "You have tested my heart; You have visited me in the night; You have tried me and have found nothing; I have purposed that my mouth shall not transgress" (Ps. 17:3).

Hit the Pause Button

Think before you speak. Choose your words carefully. Avoid using your language with the intent to hurt another. Remember: every thought that comes to mind doesn't need to come out of your mouth.

"So then, my beloved brethren, let every man be swift to hear, slow to speak, slow to wrath" (James 1:19).

Delve into Scripture

If you want to dig deeper, do a study on mentions of the mouth, words, tongue, etc. in Scripture. Just a search in Proverbs will give you a wealth of information. Once you get all that information, don't just let it sit in your head. Act on the truth.

> But be doers of the word, and not hearers only, deceiving yourselves. For if anyone is a hearer of the word and not a doer, he is like a man observing his natural face in a mirror; for he observes himself, goes away, and immediately forgets what kind of man he was. But he who looks into the perfect law of liberty and continues in it, and is not a forgetful hearer but a doer of the work, this one will be blessed in what he does. (James 1:22–25)

Based on what you have learned from this chapter, what will you commit to do? _____

_____

_____

_____

Additional Resources

War of Words by Paul Tripp

Application Questions

1. What one or two statements impacted me from this chapter?

   a. _____

   b. _____

2. How can I apply it/them to my life today and begin to pursue positive growth? _____
_____

3. What one step am I willing to take to move toward heart change in my reactions, behavior or attitude? _____
_____

4. What do I learn about God from this chapter? _____
_____

5. How does His Word (the Bible) confirm this? _____
_____
_____

7

Anger and Bitterness

by DeEtta Marsh

Get rid of all bitterness, rage, and anger, brawling and slander, along with every form of malice.
Ephesians 4:31 (NIV)

7

*W*e have all experienced anger—both as the recipient and as the perpetrator. While it is a common struggle, it can become a life-dominating issue.

Anger is a very common problem in relationships involving a person struggling with addiction. What about for you personally? Do you often find yourself angry? Have you ever reached the point of feeling like you might explode because your anger was so great and overwhelming? Read on.

Part 1: What is Anger?

Anger can be: "God-given energy to help us solve problems biblically"[1]; "A powerful emotion that is often misused to hurt others"[2]; "An emotional response to an unmet expectation or perceived injustice."[3] Jay Adams says, "Anger, like every other emotion that God has given us, is a proper and useful emotion when it is expressed in a manner that is consistent with the principles of the Scriptures and used for the purposes that God set forth in that Book."[4]

The Bible indicates that not all anger is sinful. Look up First Kings 11:9, Second Kings 17:18, Psalm 7:11 and Mark 3:5.

Who is angry in these verses? _____

Why isn't this kind of anger sinful? _____
_____

Write Ephesians 4:26: _____
_____
_____

Considering the implications of this verse, do you believe all anger is sinful? Why or why not? ____
_____
_____

Righteous anger is against the wrong, not the wrong-doer. In her article "Why Am I So Angry?" Shannon B. Rainey writes, "Righteous [or "good"] anger is aroused by hatred of sin and a passion for God's glory."[5] Unrighteous anger tends to be against a person. Although not all anger is wrong, we, as humans, most often stray into unrighteous responses to anger—whether the cause is righteous or unrighteous. Rainey continues, "Our anger at injustice can lead to sin when we seek revenge, which belongs to the Lord (Rom. 12:19), or when we refuse to forgive as the Lord has forgiven us (Col. 3:13)."

When we are offended and angry, our flesh wants to even the score—to make the other person pay for our pain. Frankly, we want revenge. We may not think of it this way, but seeking revenge is like trying to do God's job for Him, not trusting Him to avenge the wrong. Yet Romans 12:19 tells us, "Beloved, do not avenge yourselves, but rather give place to wrath; for it is written, 'Vengeance is Mine, I will repay,' says the Lord."

So what are we to do? Nothing? No, we are to "Put on tender mercies, kindness, humility, meekness, longsuffering; bearing with one another, and forgiving one another, if anyone has a complaint against another; even as Christ forgave you, so you also must do" (Col. 3:12–13).

So how can we discern if our anger is righteous or unrighteous? If you are experiencing anger over perceived injustice, ask yourself:

♦ Does my violated conviction reflect God's laws or my own legalism? _____

♦ Am I truly grieved over the affront to God's holiness, or am I more upset by how the sin affects me? _____

♦ Am I reacting to protect others or myself? _____

♦ Does my self-righteousness blind me to the fact that I too am capable of equally heinous sin?

_____

Sinful anger or unrighteous anger leads to a multitude of hurts, hatred, bitterness and strife. This type of anger is spiritually damaging because it keeps us from developing a spirit that is pleasing to God. We can get to the point of feeling like we can't control ourselves. There is hope for change, however, because unrighteous anger is a learned behavior that can be controlled when the circumstances require it. For example, have you ever been yelling at the kids, yet when the phone rings, you answer it in your sweetest voice? There are appropriate times and ways to express anger, but it is never right to do it in an ungodly, uncontrolled way.

Part 2: Anger Expressed

A person may express unrighteous anger in a couple of ways. The most common picture of anger that comes to mind is "blowing up," "letting off steam" or venting. This expression of anger is aimed at destroying people and/or things as it "releases the energies of anger, but in ways that do not really solve the problem."[6]

The other way of handling anger sinfully is "clamming up," or holding it in, instead of trying to resolve the situation. This also fails to solve the problem and often results in resentment and bitterness.

If a person has a problem with blowing up, attempting to change by clamming up will not work; neither will clamming up be solved by letting off steam. Changing behavior alone will not permanently resolve the problem, because the issue is rooted in the heart. The solution must come through God dealing with the source of the anger and helping you express it in a godly manner.

The biblical alternative to blowing up or clamming up is to "aim all your energies at solving the problem God's way."[7] When you become aware of an offense, ask God to show you constructive ways to channel your anger to help bring about positive change. Try to identify the "why?" behind your anger, and after searching your own motives, ask God to show you His way of bringing about change in your heart and the other person's as well.

First Corinthians 10:13 states, "No temptation has overtaken you except such as is common to man; but God is faithful, who will not allow you be tempted beyond what you are able, but with the temptation, will also make the way of escape, that you may be able to bear it."

God will give you everything you need to resist the temptation to express ungodly anger and to respond, by the power of His Spirit, with gentleness and grace—without dodging or ignoring the issue. Words spoken when angry must not be directed at destroying the person but at destroying the problem.

"Let no corrupt word proceed out of your mouth, but what is good for necessary edification, that it may impart grace to the hearers" (Eph. 4:29). Or, in Jay Adams's translation, "Let no unwholesome word proceed out of your mouth, but only such a word as is good for building up, aimed at the problem that has arisen, that it may give help to those who hear."[8] There is a fine line between attacking an issue and attacking your offender. Pray first; speak second.

Write Ephesians 4:31: _____

_____

_____

Which of the emotional expressions of anger do you find evident in your life? _____

_____

Let's back up a few verses to Ephesians 4:22–24: "Put off concerning your former conduct, the old man which grows corrupt according to the deceitful lusts, and be renewed in the spirit of your mind, and that you put on the new man which was created according to God, in true righteousness and holiness." God desires that you "put away" or "put off" your old reactions and expressions of anger, replacing them with the characteristics named in Ephesians 4:32: "And be kind to one another, tenderhearted, forgiving one another, even as God in Christ forgave you."

Let's put verses from Ephesians 4 into a table to bring clarity to the put off/put on principle of God's Word.

PUT OFF	PUT ON
Lying (4:25)	Speaking the truth (4:25)
Stealing (4:28)	Working with hands and giving (4:28)
Corrupt talk(4:29)	Words of edification (4:29)
Bitterness (4:31)	Forgiveness (4:32)
Anger (4:31)	Forgiveness (4:32)
Wrath (4:31)	Forgiveness (4:32)
Clamor (4:31)	Kindness (4:32)

PUT OFF	PUT ON
Evil speaking (4:31)	Kindness (4:32), words that impart grace (4:29)
Malice (4:31)	Tender-heartedness (4:32)

God is not simply looking for us to "put off" wrong behaviors; He empowers us, by the Holy Spirit, to "put on" correct behaviors.

Part 3: Getting to the Root of the Problem

Anger is something we do, not something we are. The Bible says the cause of anger is you—it comes out of your heart. "Where do wars and fights come from among you? Do they not come from your desires for pleasure that war in your members? You lust and do not have. You murder and covet and cannot obtain. You fight and war. Yet you do not have because you do not ask. You ask and do not receive, because you ask amiss, that you may spend it on your pleasures" (James 4:1–3). So, overly-simplified, anger is the result of unmet expectations, or unfulfilled desires/wants. In other words, I get angry when I don't get what I want.

In his book *Secrets of the Heart: Lessons from the Psalms*, Stuart Briscoe states, "Human beings love to think that we are in control of our lives. But when we lose control, anxiety results. Anxiety can turn into resentment. Resentment can become anger."[9]

People deal with anger in a variety of ways. Some people refuse to acknowledge their anger. Others know they're angry, but will not, or believe they cannot, express their feelings. Still others release their anger by "telling it like it is"—usually displaying a lack of self-control. Lastly, there are those who live life God's way, seeking and granting forgiveness. Which type best describes you? _____

_____

Here are some Bible verses about the *wrong* way to handle anger. What do you learn from each?

1. Proverbs 14:17, 29 _____

_____

2. Proverbs 15:1, 18 _____

_____

3. Proverbs 19:19 _____

_____

4. Proverbs 25:28 _____

_____

5. Galatians 5:15 _____

_____

6. Romans 12:17–21 _____

_____

What are some of the incorrect ways you handle anger? _____

_____

_____

How are your anger and angry reactions an offense to God? _____

_____

Write a prayer to God about your angry offenses. _____

_____

_____

_____

Ungodly anger is destructive. When we are quick-tempered or harsh with our wortds, we end up looking foolish. Responding angrily in situations only adds fuel to the harmful fire.

The following Bible verses are examples of the *right* way to handle anger. What do you learn from each?

1. Proverbs 15:1 _____

_____

2. Proverbs 16:32 _____

_____

3. Proverbs 19:11 _____

_____

4. Matthew 5:43–44 _____

_____

_____

5. Romans 12:19–21 _____

_____

6. Ephesians 4:26 _____

_____

7. Ephesians 5:20 _____

_____

8. James 1:19–20 _____

_____

_____

While anger isn't wrong in and of itself, how we deal with it can be. Ungodly anger tends to be self-serving while godly anger focuses on God and the other person. We are called to love those who anger or persecute us. If we can overlook an offense, the problem is deflated before it becomes a serious issue. If we cannot overlook the offense, then we should be slow to become angry and prompt to address the situation. We can often diffuse an argument by remaining calm and responding with a gentle spirit. It is vital to yield to the Holy Spirit's control of our lives to accomplish God's plan and purpose in each situation.

Part 4: What Are the Results of Anger?

Long-held, unresolved anger results in bitterness and resentment. When you do not repent of and resolve sinful anger, it takes root in your heart as bitterness. The cycle then continues—resentment leads to anger which leads to bitterness which leads to more resentment and more anger and more bitterness. Hebrews 12:14–15 exhorts, "Pursue peace with all people, and holiness, without which no one will see the Lord: looking carefully lest anyone fall short of the grace of God; lest any root of bitterness springing up cause trouble, and by this many become defiled." It is easier to recognize bitterness in others than in ourselves because of the deception of our hearts and our own spiritual blindness. Jeremiah 17:9 tells us, "The heart is deceitful above all things, And desperately wicked; Who can know it?" Author Beth Moore takes it a step further, "Since the root feeds the rest of the tree, every branch of our lives and every fruit on each limb ultimately becomes poisoned."[10]

Bitterness accumulates like a rolling snowball. Anger, bitterness and resentment grow larger and larger with each insult—whether real, imagined or unintentional—because of a continuous review of the details of past hurts.

A good way to tell you're bitter is if you find yourself rehashing past situations. Brooding bitterness against someone is sin, and it causes spiritual damage by keeping us from developing a spirit that is pleasing to God. Stuart Briscoe states, "If we're not careful, we can form such a habit of anger, resentment and bitterness that it becomes our pattern of life."[11]

What are some symptoms of bitterness that can be recognized when it is a life pattern? Bitterness may be manifested and observed in various ways—such as in constant complaining and nit-picking, frequent physical illnesses, depression and lethargic behavior. "Unresolved anger becomes a dark cloud over our lives." If a person does not take positive steps to resolve the real or imagined wrongs, he/she tends to become "more and more explosive, and/or more and more depressed." Bitterness is cumulative and feeds on itself; the more we practice bitterness, the more prone we are to perpetuate bitterness.

How has bitterness affected your life? _____

_____

Bitterness breeds more bitterness; the only path to healing is forgiveness. Listen: the person most hurt by your bitterness is you. We are not to be debt collectors. Failing to forgive another holds that person in debt to us, and we offend God by that attitude and behavior. "Repay no one evil for evil. Have regard for good things in the sight of all men. If it is possible, as much as depends on you, live peaceably with all men. Beloved, do not avenge yourselves, but rather give place to wrath; for it is written, 'Vengeance is Mine, I will repay,' says the Lord" (Rom. 12: 17–19). We often take upon ourselves that which only God can appropriately do—repayment. Releasing responsibility for justice to God is not a resignation that there will be no justice but rather trusting the One to whom justice belongs—God.

Make a list. On one side of the paper write down, "Who are the people that I believe have wronged me?" Beside each name write what the person has done. Be specific and detailed. Next, take this list and, one by one, release all the wrongs and emotions to God by praying about each situation and for each person. Then burn or shred the paper to signify that all the wrongs have been released to God. Choose to accept any ongoing consequences others' sins have created. (The consequences are going to remain whether you accept them or resent them, and resentment will only trap you in bitterness.)

Perhaps your anger and bitterness are toward God for things that have happened in your past, and by dwelling on them you have allowed the devil to control your life through your critical spirit. The bondage of bitterness and anger reveals "a heart set on having it my way,"[12] and it dishonors the Lord. As Gary Chapman, author of *The Other Side of Love*, reminds us, "It is never our job to vindicate ourselves by making people pay for their wrongs."[13] Genuinely releasing these hurts, injustices, betrayals and losses to God brings emotional and spiritual healing and changes us.

Write Ephesians 4:31: _____
_____
_____
_____
_____

Part 5: Freedom from Anger and Bitterness

"Bitterness shouldn't be embraced, worked through or understood—it needs to be repented of."[14] Repentance means agreeing with God about my sin and doing an "about face" in my behavior. Since bitterness feeds on negative thinking, you need to change your thought patterns.

When you choose to follow Christ, life changes. You gain the power to live differently. "This I say, therefore, and testify in the Lord, that you should *no longer walk* as the rest of the Gentiles walk, in the *futility* of their mind, having their understanding darkened, being *alienated* from the life of God, because of the ignorance that is in them, because of the *blindness of their heart*" (Eph. 4: 17–18).

You will never accidentally stumble across freedom from anger and bitterness; you will need to make intentional choices. "But you have not so learned Christ, if indeed you have heard Him and have been taught by Him, as the truth is in Jesus: that you *put off* concerning your former conduct, the old man which grows corrupt according to the deceitful lusts, and *be renewed in the spirit of your mind*, and that you put on the new man which was created according to God, in true righteousness and holiness" (Eph. 4:20–24).

Since bitterness feeds on negative thinking, one way to stop it is to meditate on God's truth, refusing to dwell on negative thoughts. "Finally, brethren, whatever things are true, whatever things are noble, whatever things are just, whatever things are pure, whatever things are lovely, whatever things are of good report, if there is any virtue and if there is anything praiseworthy—meditate on these things" (Phil. 4:8).

It is good to have a specific, biblical truth to combat every bitter thought.

Bitter Thoughts	Kind-hearted Thoughts	Biblical Truth
I could never forgive that person.	After all the Lord has forgiven me, this is the least I can do.	"Then his master after he had called him, said to him 'You wicked servant! I forgave you all that debt because you begged me. Should you not also have had compassion on your fellow servant just as I had pity on you?'" Matt. 18:32–33
God understands I can't take this anymore.	God will give me the grace and wisdom to hang in there and get through this situation. God's grace is proportional to the magnitude of my problem.	"My grace is sufficient for you, for my strength is made perfect in weakness." 2 Cor. 12:9 "But He gives more grace. Therefore He says: 'God resists the proud, but gives grace to the humble.'" James 4:6
I can't believe he did that to me.	He is a sinner in need of a Savior just like me.	"For when we were still without strength, in due time Christ died for the ungodly. . . . But God demonstrates His own love toward us, in that while we were sinners, Christ died for us." Rom. 5:6,8
I don't deserve this.	God will use this to conform me to the image of His Son.	"And we know that all things work together for good to those who love God, to those who are the called according to *His* purpose for whom He foreknew, He also predestined *to be* conformed to the image of His Son, that He might be the firstborn among many brethren." Rom. 8:28–29

Forgiveness is God's cure for bitterness and anger. Practice the habit of replacing bitter thoughts with biblical truths. Pray for the situation you're struggling with as well as for the person who hurt you— "bringing every thought into captivity to the obedience of Christ," and trusting God for the victory and healing (2 Cor. 10:5).

Additional Resources

"Changing Hearts, Changing Lives" Audio Series
CCEF Resources for Changing Lives, 1-800-318-2186

"Anger Part I: Understanding Anger" *Journal of Biblical Counseling*, Fall 1995, 42–53.
by David Powilson

"Anger Part II: Three Lies About Anger and the Transforming Truth"
Journal of Biblical Counseling, Winter 1996, 12–21.
by David Powilson

The Heart of Anger by Lou Prilio

Application Questions

1. What one or two statements impacted me from this chapter?

   a. _____

   b. _____

2. How can I apply it/them to my life today and begin to pursue positive growth? _____
   _____

3. What one step am I willing to take to move toward heart change in my reactions, behavior or attitude? _____
   _____

4. What do I learn about God from this chapter? _____
   _____

5. How does His Word (the Bible) confirm this? _____
   _____
   _____

8

Biblical Forgiveness

by Mary Ann Kiernan

Be kind and compassionate to one another, forgiving each other, just as in Christ God forgave you.

Ephesians 4:32

8

Since Adam and Eve's sin in the garden, mankind has desperately needed the forgiveness of the Creator God. Because of our sinful nature, we are not only in need of forgiveness for our sins against God—we also need to forgive others when they sin against us. Additionally, God calls us to seek forgiveness from others when we sin against them. This is not easy for us to understand or to put into practice. Everett L. Worthington says, "The concept of forgiveness is as slippery as a greased watermelon in a swimming pool. The harder you squeeze it, the more slippery it becomes."[1] As fallen humans, we struggle with forgiveness, especially when we have been deeply hurt. Forgiveness is a superhuman undertaking.

Hurt and pain occur in every relationship—it's unavoidable. But when you add addiction to that relationship, the hurt goes deeper and becomes an ongoing, repetitive ache. So what do you do when you're overwhelmed with suffering and feel that it is the result of someone else's actions? In this chapter we will wrestle with what it means to forgive biblically and to put on the *forgiving lifestyle* that Scripture calls us to practice.

> Therefore, as the elect of God, holy and beloved, put on tender mercies, kindness, humility, meekness, longsuffering; bearing with one another, and forgiving one another, if anyone has a complaint against another; even as Christ forgave you, so you also must do. But above all these things put on love, which is the bond of perfection. (Col. 3:12–14)

What do you learn about forgiveness from this passage? _____
_____
_____

God calls us to forgive whatever grievances we have against others—no matter how deep the pain—and He doesn't provide any option other than forgiveness. Of course, the more we learn about forgiveness, the more impossible it seems to accomplish. But the good news is that God promises us *the power to forgive through the Holy Spirit living in us!* When you genuinely forgive from your heart in obedience to God, you will be able to move past all your pain and live in true freedom.

"But You are God, ready to pardon, gracious and merciful, slow to anger, abundant in kindness, and did not forsake them" (Neh. 9:17). What does this verse tell you about the nature of God? _____
_____
_____

It would be impossible to talk about forgiveness and leave out love. One can't exist without the other, and the two are bound together in God. It is only because of God's great love for us that He provided a way for forgiveness. Write out John 3:16: _____

Jesus is our ultimate example of obedience, forgiveness and love. In His three-year ministry on earth, Jesus modeled a forgiving lifestyle for us through His teaching, His parables and those He forgave, and His ultimate example of forgiveness was through His death and suffering for you and me on the cross. Ephesians 4:32 commands us, "And be kind to one another, tenderhearted, forgiving one another, even as God in Christ forgave you."

That's not to say that love and forgiveness are *easy*; it's hard to accept that we must, in obedience to God, forgive those who have hurt us because of what Christ did on the cross for us. We think it's easy for God to forgive because, well, *He's God*, so we tend to think He surely can't expect *us* to do the same. Yet Matthew 6:14 reminds us, "For if you forgive men their trespasses, your heavenly Father will also forgive you."

So what does it mean to forgive? How do you define forgiveness? _____
_____
_____
_____
_____
_____

According to Merriam-Webster, "forgiveness" is "to give up resentment of or claim to requital" as in "*forgive* an insult"; "to grant relief from payment" as in "*forgive* a debt"; or " to cease to feel resentment against (an offender)."[2] Simply put, when I forgive someone who has hurt me, I cancel the debt, give up all my rights to seek revenge against that person and choose to respond in love.

Forgiveness means choosing to forgive others in the same way that God forgives us. God does not stay angry; rather He pardons, shows mercy, has compassion and chooses not to remember our sin when we confess and repent. "If we confess our sins, He is faithful and just to forgive us our sins and to cleanse us from all unrighteousness" (1 John 1:9).

If we look at Scripture from the point of man's fall in the garden to the substitutionary death of Christ, we note that thousands of years passed before the sin issue was resolved. God could have sent Jesus a short time after Adam and Eve first sinned, but He didn't. It's not that God couldn't decide whether or not to pardon mankind. Forgiveness was always His plan; He just worked it out in His time. Through God's process of forgiveness, He proved that there's nothing we could do on our own to be forgiven. God wanted us to understand the seriousness of sin. Even though God made a covenant with Abraham and gave the Law through Moses, man was still lost in his sinfulness. Then God sent His Son, and in obedience to the Father, Jesus chose to pay our debt of sin by dying on the cross. As a result, we are free from the bondage of sin.

You must *choose* to forgive in the same way God chose to send His son and Christ chose to die to redeem us. Mathew 6:14–15 tells us, "For if you forgive men their trespasses, your heavenly Father will also forgive you. But if you do not forgive men their trespasses, neither will your Father forgive your trespasses." In what way does this passage depict forgiveness as a choice? _____

When you are sinned against, you have a clear choice to make. You may want to respond with revenge—by hurting the person who wronged you[3]—but Luke reminds us, "Judge not, and you shall not be judged. Condemn not, and you shall not be condemned. Forgive, and you will be forgiven" (6:37). Dr. Grace Ketterman and David Hazard explain, "Forgiveness is an unnatural act for us but a natural one for God. What seems natural and almost instantaneous when we are hurt is revenge. We immediately want to respond by hurting the other person in some way."[3]

Romans 12:18–19 commands us, "If it is possible, as much as depends on you, live peaceably with all men. Beloved, do not avenge yourselves, but rather give place to wrath; for it is written, 'Vengeance is Mine, I will repay,' says the Lord."

Based on the above verse, if you forgive, does the person who hurt you "get away with it"? If yes, how? If no, why not? _____

_____

Leaving revenge and wrath in God's hands doesn't mean the offender won't face consequences. It isn't up to us to try to take God's place and try to be judge, jury and punishment enforcer. We may feel justified in our actions and feelings, knowing the other deserves to be judged for his/her sin against us. And yes, someday that person will have to answer for what he/she has done, and we may even derive some satisfaction from that. But it isn't just about the other person. Matthew 7:2 states, "For with what judgment you judge, you will be judged; and with the measure you use, it will be measured back to you." What about us? "For we must all appear before the judgment seat of Christ, that each one may receive the things done in the body, according to what he has done, whether good or bad" (2 Cor. 5:10). We often don't think about how God sees our reactions when we feel like victims, but we need to prayerfully consider our responses to those we feel have wronged us. I like the way *The Message* says it: "So where does that leave you when you criticize a brother? And where does that leave you when you condescend to a sister? I'd say it leaves you looking pretty silly—or worse. Eventually, we're all going to end up kneeling side by side in the place of judgment, facing God. Your critical and condescending ways aren't going to improve your position there one bit." (Rom. 14: 10–12).

Your response when someone sins against you is extremely important. God commands that we not only choose to *forgive* but that we choose to *love* those that have hurt us—no matter what they've done. This is not easy to accept in our flesh. So what does God's Word tell us to do? "Therefore, as the elect of God, holy and beloved, put on tender mercies, kindness, humility, meekness, longsuffering; bearing with one another, and forgiving one another, if anyone has a complaint against another; even as Christ forgave you, so you also must do" (Col. 3:12–13) and "You ought rather to forgive and comfort him, lest perhaps such a one be swallowed up with too much sorrow. Therefore I urge you to reaffirm your love for him" (2 Cor. 2:7–8). These verses explain you ought to forgive and even *comfort* your offender; to keep him from sorrow, you should "reaffirm your love for him." Right about now, you probably want to rip this chapter right out of your book, because showing love probably goes against all your natural reactions of anger. But please don't give up. Pray for God to give you a deeper understanding and to fill you with His Holy Spirit so you can do whatever He asks of you.

What are some reasons forgiveness is difficult for you? _____

_____

_____

Read Matthew 18:21–35. What are the critical points of this passage? _____

_____

_____

According to this Scripture, why should you forgive someone who has hurt you? _____

_____

_____

What are some of the things for which God has stamped "paid in full" on your account? _____

_____

_____

What are some sins you had a difficult time forgiving or have not yet forgiven? _____

_____

_____

_____

We often fail to forgive because deep down we don't believe the offense should be pardoned. When we look at events like the mass murder at the Virginia Polytechnic Institute and State University in 2007, the killings of ten Amish school girls in Pennsylvania in 2006, the cruel acts of the serial killers "the Son of Sam" and Jeffrey Dahmer, and the incomparably inhumane acts of Hitler and his regime, we cry out to God, "Lord, surely we aren't meant to forgive *these* people in these types of circumstances!"

Or maybe, to bring it closer to home, you've struggled with forgiving someone for infidelity, lies upon lies, abandonment, abuse—and the list goes on. "Really, God? You can't possibly expect me to forgive these sins too!" you cry. Yet Matthew 6:14–15 says that *anytime* someone sins against us, we are to forgive them. There is no distinction to the degree of hurt; big or small, we are to forgive it *all*, and this even extends to the person who hurts us again and again (Matt. 18:21–22).

If this seems overwhelming and you are having difficulty understanding and accepting the necessity of forgiveness, take time now to cry out to God. Ask for a willing heart to forgive, a deeper understanding of Scripture, the courage to choose to forgive and the power of the Holy Spirit to make it all happen.

Forgiveness Myths and Misconceptions

Myth 1: Being unforgiving gives you power over the person who hurt you.

✧ When you refuse to forgive, you give power over your life to another individual. Chains of unforgivingness bind you and affect all areas of your life—emotionally, physically and spiritually.

✧ It is easy to get stuck in a "victim mentality" rather than to live in victory through Christ. The underlying message of the "victim mentality" is "I am like this because of what that person has done to me. I can't change unless he changes"—but Christ did not call us to sort through all our earthly relationships before obeying His word. We are to forgive, not complain and complicate. Sometimes we walk around ready to show our wounds to anyone who will look so they can know our pain and can perhaps comfort or sympathize with us. We basically carry a placard proclaiming we've been betrayed, abandoned, cheated on, abused (physically or emotionally), etc.—you can fill in the blank. But this never solves our problem; in fact, it tends to keep the wounds raw and painful.

✧ We have a tendency to first take our hurts to our family or friends and then at some point go to God, but our heavenly Father waits for us to bring all our wounds to Him. His arms are opened wide, ready to comfort and give us His strength. He tells us, "Come to Me, all you who labor and are heavy laden, and I will give you rest. Take My yoke upon you and learn from Me, for I am gentle and lowly in heart, and you will find rest for your souls. For My yoke is easy and My burden is light" (Matt. 11:28–30). He is the only One who will listen at any time, night or day. He is the only One who can truly comfort us. He's the One who stands ready to take us from victim to victor. We may not forget what has happened, but God takes our pain, hurts and suffering and transforms them to treasure for His glory. We can claim victory through Christ. Our pain no longer defines who we are; rather the event and the hurt are included in the fabric of our lives to grow us into a stronger character. It has been said that being unforgiving is like taking poison and expecting the other person to die; this attitude has powerful negative affects on your physical, emotional and spiritual well-being. Unforgivingness and bitterness go hand in hand, and their roots grow very deep. They will affect all other relationships in your life—especially your relationship with God.

✧ Contrastingly, biblical forgiveness sets you free. Other people may be responsible for pain in your life, but you can either choose to allow the pain to damage your present and future, or you can choose to forgive and be set free. "Pursue peace with all people, and holiness, without which no one will see the Lord: looking carefully lest anyone fall short of the grace of God; lest any root of bitterness springing up cause trouble, and by this many become defiled" (Heb. 12:14–15).

Myth 2: If you forgive, you make yourself a doormat for your offender to hurt you again and take advantage of you.

✧ Being forgiving doesn't remove the necessity of acting wisely and with discernment. We are at all times to seek the Lord's knowledge and understanding so that we might recognize true justice. Proverbs tells us, "My son, if you receive my words, and treasure my commands within you, so that you incline your ear to wisdom, and apply your heart to understanding; yes, if you cry out for discernment, and lift up your voice for understanding, if you seek her as silver, and search for her as for hidden treasures; then you will understand the fear of the LORD, and find the knowledge of God. For the LORD gives wisdom; from His mouth come knowledge and understanding; He stores up sound wisdom for the upright; He is a shield to those who walk uprightly; He guards the paths of justice, and preserves the way of His saints. Then you will understand righteousness and justice, equity and every good path" (2:1–9).

✧ Forgiveness does not remove the consequences of the offense. Galatians 6:7 says, "A man reaps what he sows" (NIV). If you take away natural consequences of a person's actions, you may be robbing your offender of God's discipline, of valuable lessons that God has planned for them and of the possibility of repentance. You can't judge others and either give pardon or impose punishment—that's God's job. Pray for the Lord to reveal to you His good and perfect will and justice. "Blessed is the man whom You instruct, O LORD, and teach out of Your law" (Ps. 94:12).

✧ Write out Romans 12:17–19: _____

_____

_____

✧ Write out Matthew 7:1–2: _____

_____

_____

_____

✧ Forgiveness and trust are not the same thing. *Forgiveness* is free; *trust* must be earned. When you forgive you do not need to automatically trust the person again. Trust takes time to be restored.

Myth 3: If you forgive, you must forget.

✧ God never *forgets* (as in ceases to remember) sin when He forgives. If that were true, He would not be omniscient. However, God does *choose* not to remember our sins, and He keeps no record of our wrongs (Ps. 130:3). Or look at Joseph: he recalled his brothers' sin against him yet spoke lovingly to them. (Gen. 50:19–21). When you forgive, you don't forget the pain or the event, but you make the choice to move on.

✧ Even in the midst of your pain, there are still valuable lessons for you to learn. You can't hold out for your offender to apologize and promise to change before you offer forgiveness. Joseph's brothers didn't ask for his forgiveness nor did he see any changes in them, yet he pardoned them.

✧ Read Genesis 45:1–15. What was Joseph's response to his brothers? _____

_____

✧ Read the account of the prodigal son in Luke 15:11–32. What was the father's response when he saw his son? _____

_____

✧ What do you learn from God in these two accounts that dispel the myth that forgiveness necessitates forgetfulness? _____

_____

_____

Myth 4: Forgiveness is a one-time action; you pardon the offense, and then you're done forever.

✧ Forgiveness is a *process* that begins when you make the choice to forgive. The deeper your hurt, the harder it is to forgive, but it is never impossible. Your process may require that you remember your choice to forgive daily, hourly or even moment by moment.

✧ Even though your hurt may be very deep and the forgiving process may take some time, you should eventually reach a place of release and peace. Forgiveness should never take a lifetime, no matter how serious the hurt.[4] You may need to enlist the help of your pastor or a biblical counselor.

Myth 5: You need to forgive God for the hurt you have suffered in your life.

✧ This concept is not found anywhere in the Bible; no one is ever called to forgive God. There are examples of people who were angry at God for their suffering (see the Psalms) or angry because God hadn't given them the answer to why they were suffering. Job suffered great loss, pain and depression. He became angry at God, and he wanted—or actually demanded—answers. Job even tried to blame God for his suffering: "Know then that God has wronged me, and has surrounded me with His net. If I cry out concerning wrong, I am not heard. If I cry aloud, there is no justice" (Job 19:6–7). What is

God's response? (Job 40:1–14) _____

_____

_____

✧ Read Job 42:1–6. What does Job come to understand is the answer to his anger and to his questions of why he has suffered so much? _____

_____

_____

✧ You see, you do not need to forgive God because God has never sinned against you; He has never done any wrong to you. We must purpose to have a deeper understanding of God's character and nature and must repent of our own sin. Only when we are silenced by our own sin and stunned by God's response to our hatred will our hearts be able to forgive, love and have compassion for those who have hurt us. Forgiveness allows us to understand both the heart of God and what He was willing to pay for our forgiveness.

Myth 6: You need to forgive yourself.

✧ Forgiving yourself, far from something that is biblically commanded, is a concept that came from the secular world and has begun to infiltrate some churches. Jesus forgave sins and admonished those He forgave to "go and sin no more" (John 8:11)—He never prescribed forgiving oneself.

✧ Feeling pain over what you have done—rather than being "unforgiving" of yourself—is regret. Regret is sometimes mislabeled as not *feeling* forgiven, but regret can be a good emotion because it can help to build compassion for others and humility in our hearts.[5]

✧ Once you have asked God and the person you sinned against for forgiveness, you must let the issue go and allow the blood of Jesus to cleanse *all* your sin. (Read Mark 2:5; Psalm 103:12; Isaiah 1:18; 38:17; 43:25; 44:22 and Micah 7:19.)

✧ Believing you can forgive yourself makes you your own judge! "The self-forgiveness notion strangely views the one person as the offender, the judge and the forgiver."[6] But God is the only one who judges and forgives.

✧ When feelings of pain, regret or guilt creep into your thinking, take time to stop and think about God's forgiveness of you and give thanks for the blood of Christ that has covered your sin.

The Forgiving Lifestyle

As you process what you have learned so far, ask yourself this question: Why would I choose to forgive? (See Luke 11:2–4 and Mark 11:25–26.) _____

_____

Biblical forgiveness sets you free. Harboring bitterness and refusing to forgive is like building a prison around you brick by brick. Unforgiveness hardens your heart. It not only affects your relationship with the person who has hurt you but complicates other relationships as well. It stunts your spiritual growth and puts a wall between you and the Lord.

How has being unforgiving affected your relationship with God? With others? _____

_____

In our flesh we think that the price should be paid by the person who hurt us; however, if Jesus is our example of a forgiving lifestyle, we as His followers recognize that we pay *no* price and carry *no* debt for our sins. The price of forgiveness is always paid by the one doing the forgiving.

Take the time to write out a prayer of thanksgiving to Jesus for the ultimate sacrifice He made for you and the freedom you have from carrying the debt of your sin. _____

_____

_____

What Does a Forgiving Lifestyle Look Like?

✧ You make the choice not to talk about the person who has hurt you or the event itself. (Read Ephesians 4:29.)

✧ You make a choice not to bring up the hurt or event to the person who has sinned against you once it has been forgiven.

✧ You make a choice not play all the old hurt tapes in your head. Revisiting the pain only leads to more anger, hurt and bitterness—never to healing and freedom. You may not be able to stop the first thought, but you can stop the second.[7] Even if the thoughts come to mind, you can examine and test your thoughts against Scripture. Philippians 4:8 exhorts, "Finally, brethren, whatever things are true, whatever things are noble, whatever things are just, whatever things are pure, whatever things are lovely, whatever things are of good report, if there is any virtue and if there is anything praiseworthy—meditate on these things."

✧ You are very careful with whom you share your hurt. It may be necessary to talk with someone—a pastor, biblical counselor, or even a trusted Christian friend—who will not jump on your bandwagon but will speak love and truth into your life.

✧ You don't allow the event to stand between you and the person who hurt you. (Of course, sometimes boundaries must be set in place. And just because you're working to restore relationship does not mean that all consequences for the action are removed.)

✧ Your deep desire in forgiving is to see the person who sinned against you be reconciled with God—which might include encountering the saving knowledge of Jesus Christ for the first time—because this is God's desire. "For this is good and acceptable in the sight of God our Savior, who desires all men to be saved and to come to the knowledge of the truth" (1 Tim. 2:3–4).

✧ If you are the one who has sinned against another, you actively seek to resolve the issue quickly—seeking God's forgiveness and asking forgiveness of the person you have hurt. In what ways and to whom do you recognize yourself as an offender? _____

_____

_____

The Process of Forgiveness

1. Begin by making the choice to forgive in obedience to God (Matt. 18:32–35; Luke 7:47; John 8:7;

Rom. 12:14–16). There may be some very deep hurt in your life, and you may honestly wrestle with this choice. You will need to cry out to God and ask Him to make you willing to forgive.

What are some of the obstacles that stand in the way of your making the choice to forgive? _____
_____
_____
_____

Forgiveness requires that you look at the person who has hurt you through the lens of Scripture. Ask God to open the eyes of your heart so that you might see your offender the same way God sees him—a sinner in need of forgiveness. The more you see the person from God's perspective, the easier it will be to forgive and move on—trusting God in and through the process.[9] Paul writes in Ephesians,

> Let no corrupt communication proceed out of your mouth, but that which is good to the use of edifying, that it may minister grace unto the hearers. And grieve not the Holy Spirit of God, whereby ye are sealed unto the day of redemption. Let all bitterness, and wrath, and anger, and clamour, and evil speaking, be put away from you, with all malice: And be ye kind one to another, tenderhearted, forgiving one another, even as God for Christ's sake hath forgiven you. (4:29–32, KJV)

I love the way the King James Version renders these verses. When you forgive, you "minister grace" into the life of the one who has hurt you! You give your offender a small taste of the grace God has shown you.

2. Choose to work on and be committed to the process of forgiveness. Remember that forgiveness and love go hand in hand—you can't have one without the other. (Read Luke 7:40–48.) A forgiven person loves much and loves sacrificially in view of the great love and sacrifice of Jesus. This means you leave your issue in God's hands rather than seeking revenge.

Write out Romans 12:19: _____
_____
_____
_____

If you continue to have difficulty in choosing to forgive, the solution is to have a deeper understanding of God's forgiveness for you. Many times we attach a certain meaning to the hurt we have undergone, and this can cripple us for life. You may, in your bitterness, conclude that God is not trustworthy, that all men are liars, that you are unlovable, etc. Do not listen to Satan's lies. Seek instead to look at the meaning of your pain through Scripture's lens to see how God understands your pain and suffering.

What are some lies that block forgiveness in your life? _____
_____
_____
_____

Read Genesis 45:4–5. Joseph was able to see his suffering through the eyes of a sovereign God.

Joseph's understanding didn't come immediately, yet it did come as he was faithfully obedient and as he strove to forgive.

3. You need to take time to make an *accurate* assessment of the hurt against you and the damage that resulted from it. Do not exaggerate the offense nor minimize it. This will take a lot of courage because you will reopen your wounds as you remember your pain. But remember that God will be with you every step of the way and will comfort you and never leave you. "The LORD is near to those who have a broken heart, and saves such as have a contrite spirit" (Ps. 34:18).

   During this time it is very important not to confront the person who hurt you; instead this is a time for you to spend in prayer, seeking comfort, wisdom and discernment from God. If you have trouble staying away from the person, seek out an accountability partner to help you.

4. After making an accurate assessment of the offense, you will need to take time to grieve over the pain and loss you have experienced. Some losses may be permanent or life-changing, so they'll need to be accepted, grieved, consoled and given over to the Lord.

   Let's consider some biblical examples of dealing with loss. Read the accounts of Joseph's father, Jacob, in Genesis 37:34–35 and of Joseph in Genesis 41:50–52. Each of these men had a heavy burden of grief.

   How did they face their grief, and what difference did it make in their lives? _____
   _____
   _____
   _____
   _____

   What losses are you grieving at this time? _____
   _____
   _____

5. Learn from the past. In the eyes of God nothing is wasted—not even our pain, sorrow and suffering. Use the lessons learned from your painful experience to make better choices in your present and future. (These lessons will also help you establish loving boundaries if necessary.)

   Your experience can help you gain wisdom. "Get wisdom! Get understanding! Do not forget, nor turn away from the words of my mouth. Do not forsake her, and she will preserve you; love her, and she will keep you. Wisdom is the principal thing; therefore get wisdom. And in all your getting, get understanding" (Prov. 4:5–7).

   As you gain wisdom, you become better equpped to make decisions with discernment. "For wisdom is better than rubies, and all the things one may desire cannot be compared with her. I, wisdom, dwell with prudence, and find out knowledge and discretion" (Prov. 8:11–12).

   Remember that God is at work through all your life's circumstances. "And we know that all things work together for good to those who love God, to those who are the called according to His purpose" (Rom. 8:28).

6. Thank God for His forgiveness of your sin and worship Him. God tells us to be thankful no matter what we go through. See Philippians 4:6–7 and First Thessalonians 5:17–18. Write out your prayer of worship and thanksgiving. This should be an ongoing process as you travel the road of forgiveness. _____
   _____
   _____
   _____
   _____
   _____
   _____

7. Face the person who has hurt you. You will need God's wisdom to help you discern when you should speak up and when you need to keep silent. Dealing with those who have hurt us should always be done prayerfully and thoughtfully. Pray for those who have sinned against you. Jesus gave us this example when He hung on the cross and prayed, "Father, forgive them, for they do not know what they do" (Luke 23:34). Stephen also prayed for the very people who were stoning him. Stephen's last words are recorded in Acts 7:60: "Then he knelt down and cried out with a loud voice, 'Lord, do not charge them with this sin.' And when he had said this, he fell asleep."

   When forgiveness is given and acknowledged, it can break down walls and open doors, making a way for a more honest, loving and growing relationship. When God forgives us, it leads to a restored relationship, but this is not always the case in human relationships. It may be that you forgive someone, but the person never acknowledges his sin against you, so restoration never takes place. In Second Samuel 14:25–33 and 15:1–12, we read that King David forgave his son, Absalom with a kiss. However, no repentance or reconciliation ever took place; in fact, Absalom then conspired to take over David's throne.

   Forgiveness does not equal reconciliation. It takes one to forgive and two to reconcile.

   Take a moment now to lift up in prayer by name those who have hurt you. Write down initials and some notes as you pray. _____
   _____
   _____
   _____

8. Forgive and then don't bring up the offense again. It's not that you develop amnesia but that you make a conscious decision not to rehash the issue with the person who sinned against you.

   We have been separated from our sins (Ps. 103:12), so we ought to also pardon and free those who have sinned against us. Look at God's example of forgiveness in Hebrews 8:12: "For I will be merciful to their unrighteousness, and their sins and their lawless deeds I will remember no more."

9. Share what God has done in your life through His forgiving character so that you might give hope and comfort to others who may be struggling to forgive. It may take some time to get to this point in the process, but what rejoicing there will be when you do!

"Let your light so shine before men, that they may see your good works and glorify your Father in heaven" (Matt. 5:16).

"Blessed be the God and Father of our Lord Jesus Christ, the Father of mercies and God of all comfort, who comforts us in all our tribulation, that we may be able to comfort those who are in any trouble, with the comfort with which we ourselves are comforted by God. For as the sufferings of Christ abound in us, so our consolation also abounds through Christ" (2 Cor. 1:3–5).

10. Sometimes you may have a thought that reminds you of the offense and the pain. You may mistakenly think that you haven't forgiven them. This is the time for you remember that you have chosen to forgive and have already forgiven the person. Take the time to reflect on how God has forgiven you for your sins. Then praise God for forgiving you and praise God that you have forgiven your offender.[8] Test your thoughts against Philippians 4:8.

Living a Forgiving Lifestyle When You're the Offender

There are always two sinners in every relationship; each person has the potential to sin against the other. We tend to place the responsibility for our hurt entirely on the other person when typically we deserve some of the blame. Instead of recognizing that "all have sinned and fallen short of the glory of God" (Rom. 3:23), we consider ourselves above our offender; yet there are, of course, times in which we are responsible for sinning against someone else. So what do you do when you are the offender?

✧ Pray and ask God to reveal any sin in your heart that you may have covered over or may have justified in response to your hurt. "Search me, O God, and know my heart; try me, and know my anxieties; and see if there is any wicked way in me, and lead me in the way everlasting" (Ps. 139:23–24).

✧ Repent and confess your sin to God. "If we confess our sins, He is faithful and just to forgive us our sins and to cleanse us from all unrighteousness" (1 John 1:9). If you are having difficulty, go to a pastor, biblical counselor or a godly friend to guide, advise and help you in the process. "Confess your trespasses to one another, and pray for one another, that you may be healed. The effective, fervent prayer of a righteous man avails much" (James 5:16). Often people go to the person they have sinned against and say, "I apologize but . . ." But what is an apology? Is it the same thing as forgiveness? Merriam-Webster defines "apology" as "a formal justification, a defense" or as an "excuse."[9] When you apologize, you express your regret. An apology is appropriate for a mistake (like stepping on someone's toes). Offering an apology when you have sinned against another person is often a result of feeling badly about what happened but not necessarily being repentant over your sin. Asking for forgiveness, however, is admitting that you have sinned against God and the other person. When you ask for forgiveness, don't claim any rights or try to justify your actions. When you recognize the weight of your sin and ask the person you have sinned against to forgive you, you reveal a repentant, broken and undemanding heart.

✧ Before going to the person you sinned against, examine your heart and motives before the Lord. Are you still trying to make your point? Are you trying to avoid consequences? Are you trying to hurt the other person again by rehashing the incident? Remember, "The sacrifices of God are a broken spirit, a broken and a contrite heart—these, O God, You will not despise" (Ps. 51:17).

✧ When God forgives your sin, it leads to restoration of relationship. However, there may be times when you ask for forgiveness but the person will not forgive, and the relationship may not be restored.

✧ Realize God is in control and you are not; then enjoy the freedom.

✧ Repent—or be genuinely and sincerely sorry for your sin. Then purpose to do things differently in the future.

I imagine this study on forgiveness has been a difficult one. Remember that forgiveness is a superhuman task that can't be done in your own strength. You need the power of the Holy Spirit and the support of other people in your life to encourage you, hold you accountable and challenge you.

We often see our today through the lens of yesterday. If we don't forgive, we get stuck in the past, and we can't move forward, heal and have a victorious Christian life. This doesn't change the fact that, because of a sin against us or perhaps because of our own sin, our lives may never be the same. Our lives may have been forever altered. In view of this you must:

✧ Accept the truth of your new reality, your "new normal."
✧ Accept the fact that others in your life aren't perfect, and you aren't either.
✧ Accept that loss and pain are a part of this life here on earth.
✧ Live in freedom through the power of the Holy Spirit!

Additional Resources

The Art of Forgiving by Lewis Smedes

One Day at a Time: The Devotional for Overcomers by Neil Anderson and Mike and Julia Quarles

The Peacemaker by Ken Sande

Lord, Heal My Hurts by Kay Arthur

The Healing Power of Forgiveness by Ray Pritchard

When you Can't Say "I Forgive You" by Dr. Grace Ketterman and David Hazard

How to Cultivate Forgiveness in Your Relationships by Dr. Kevin Huggins

Bold Love by Dr. Dan B. Allender and Dr. Tremper Longman III

Application Questions

1. What one or two statements impacted me from this chapter?

   a. _____

   b. _____

2. How can I apply it/them to my life today and begin to pursue positive growth? _____
   _____

3. What one step am I willing to take to move toward heart change in my reactions, behavior or attitude? _____
   _____

4. What do I learn about God from this chapter? _____
   _____

5. How does His Word (the Bible) confirm this? _____
   _____
   _____

9

Worry, Anxiety and Fear

by Diane Hunt

Do not be anxious about anything, but in everything, by prayer and petition, with thanksgiving, present your requests to God. And the peace of God, which transcends all understanding will guard your hearts and minds in Christ Jesus.

Philippians 4:6–7, NIV

9

Life is full of events and circumstances that can rob you of your peace and joy—if you allow them. "Fear, worry, and anxiety are sins which can paralyze your mind, immobilize your body, and hinder your growth in Christ. Adam and Eve initially committed these sins in the Garden of Eden after believing Satan's lies and subsequently choosing to disobey God. Satan, not God, is behind these obstacles to spiritual maturity; but God has graciously given you all that is necessary to overcome them."[1]

Anxiety, depression and chemical abuse are the top three emotional/mental health issues today, in that order.[2] Among women affected by the life-dominating sin of addiction, anxiety is a very common problem. Let's turn to the Scriptures to see what God says about worry.

Perhaps the most familiar passage of Scripture concerning worry is Matthew 6:25–34. Take a few moments to read it now. What two analogies does Jesus use in 6:25 to make His point? _____

_____

_____

_____

What two things does Jesus want us to know from the illustration of the birds of the air? (See 6:26–27.)

_____

_____

_____

In the analogy about the lilies of the fields, Jesus speaks of the abundance of His Father's provision: "Yet I tell you that not even Solomon in all his splendor was dressed as one of these." Jesus continues, concerning the brevity of the lilies' beauty, "If that is how God clothes the grass of the field, which is here today and tomorrow is thrown into the fire . . ." (NIV). How much more will God provide for you, His own child, whom He has redeemed with the blood of His Son Jesus, a very precious price to pay?

What kind of person chases after the things in life? (6:32) _____

_____

_____

Why do you *not* need to chase after these things? (6:32) _____

_____

_____

Whenever God tells us in Scripture to stop doing something, He always tells us what to do instead. He never leaves us hanging.

What does Jesus say we are not to do? (6:31) _____
_____

Instead of that what are we to do? (6:33) _____
_____
_____

What are some practical ways for you to "seek first His kingdom and His righteousness" (Matt. 6:33, NIV) today? This week? This month? _____
_____
_____
_____
_____

Worry is always in the future tense. While often rooted in one's history or past life experiences, worry involves undue concern for the future.

> Both anxiety and worry spring from natural and legitimate concerns that are part of life in this world. But legitimate concerns are handled wrongly when they do one or more of the following: (1) become dominating concerns in our life and lead to fear, (2) destroy our perspective on life and cause us to forget that God exists and cares, or (3) move us to drift into an attitude of constant worry and concern over a future we cannot control.[3]

The common phrase "one day at a time" applies no more pointedly than with regards to worry. Jesus even tells us so in Matthew 6:34. Why do we not need to worry about tomorrow? _____
_____
_____

An all-too-familiar question asked by the worried mind is "What if. . . ?" What if I get sick? What if I lose my job? What if he fails? What if I can't pay my bills? What if we lose the house? What if I go crazy? What if my parents won't speak to me? The "what if" question will have you stressed, worried, fearful and running in circles. But that question has an answer that few of us ever remember: What if. . . ? Then God will. . . !

God's grace is enough for every situation. "My grace is sufficient for you, for My strength is made perfect in weakness" (2 Cor. 12:9). Worrying about something will give you no more control over that situation. Biblical counselor Lidia Mocelo says, "Fear begins with the belief that I am no longer in control. Faith begins with the belief that my loving, heavenly Father is in control."[4]

Read First John 4:18. What casts out all fear? _____
_____

Whose love has to be perfect for fear to be cast out? _____
_____

Refer back to 1 John 4:16. When you realize that God alone is in control of your life and that He perfectly loves you, doesn't that inspire faith and gratitude? How does this thankfulness and trust impact your worry? _____

_____

Read Paul's wonderful exhortation about worry in Philippians 4:6–7.

We are not to be anxious about anything; instead, we should pray about everything with a heart of thanksgiving. When we are fearful we pray, pray and pray some more, but there is one component that is most often neglected in our prayer. What component do you think this is? _____

_____

We often forget to pray and give thanks because we don't *feel* thankful, yet Ephesians 5:20 calls us to be continually "giving thanks always for all things to God the Father in the name of our Lord Jesus Christ." What can you be thankful for in your current circumstance? _____

_____

_____

What is the opposite of anxiety or worry? _____

What does God promise is yours in Christ when you implement Philippians 4:6–7? _____

_____

Our human tendency is to "try" what the Bible says, and if it doesn't get the desired results immediately, we give up. Don't *try* obedience—be committed to it. If you pray according to Philippians 4:6–7, but you are still anxious, keep doing it until you experience victory. Claim His promise. Believe it even if you don't *feel* it.

Write Philippians 4:6–7 on a 3x5 card. Memorize it. Frequently remind yourself of these truths:

1. Be anxious for nothing.
2. Pray with thanksgiving.
3. Make requests to God.
4. God's peace will keep my heart and mind in Christ Jesus.

Another great Scripture about anxiety is First Peter 5:6–7: "Humble yourselves, therefore, under God's almighty hand, that he may lift you up in due time. Cast all your anxiety on him because he cares for you" (NIV). Let's look at verse 7 first. In your own thinking what is implied by the word "cast?" _____

_____

What would you personally have to do to cast all your anxiety upon the Lord? _____

_____

_____

Do your struggles seem to keep coming back—even though you have released them to God? Well, when you give a problem to God, do you sit around waiting to see if it comes back, or do you fill your mind with the promises of God? Consider Second Peter 1:3–4 and Philippians 4:8. What insights do these verses give you? _____

_____

_____

_____

Second, do you really trust God with your problems? Is there a part of you that is fearful of *how* He will handle it? Are you fearful that He will not take care of it the way you want Him to?

Write Second Timothy 1:12: _____

_____

What assurance does this verse offer? _____

_____

Return to First Peter 5:6–7. Verse 6 reads, "Humble yourselves under the mighty hand of God, that He may exalt you in due time." To humble yourself under God's mighty hand requires that you submit to His plan for your life, *whatever it may be*. Do your desire to control your situation and your pride in wanting things to go *your way* become obstacles that hinder God from lifting you up? Do you really believe that His way is better than your way? How does your life reflect that truth? _____

_____

_____

_____

_____

Let's review what we have learned so far:

- ✧ Worry is not trusting God and is therefore sinful.
- ✧ We are commanded not to worry.
- ✧ Instead of worrying, we are to "seek first the kingdom of God and His righteousness" (Matt. 6:33). We are to cast all our cares on Jesus because He cares for us.
- ✧ A vital component of effective prayer and a cure for worry is thanksgiving.

When you are worried and anxious, it reflects what you believe in your heart. The *NIV Study Bible* defines the heart as "the center of the human spirit, from which spring emotions, thought, motivations, courage and action."[5] What you believe will drive your behavior and your thoughts.

Write Proverbs 27:19: _____

_____

What does this verse mean? _____

_____

_____

Matthew 12:34 says, "For out of the abundance of the heart the mouth speaks." What you *believe in your heart* will determine what you think, say and do. That does not say, what you *know* will determine what you think, say and do. "We act upon what we believe not upon what we know."[6]

So on what are you placing your belief? Let's briefly discuss three possible root causes to your worry.

Lack of Trust in God

Is God trustworthy? _____ Do you trust Him? _____

Does your life evidence that you trust God? _____

Trusting God is not about words but resting. Are you resting in Him? Are you at peace? _____
_____

Read Proverbs 3:5–6. What are you to trust God with, and what aren't you to do? _____
_____
_____

What do you do that demonstrates that you are leaning on your own understanding? _____
_____

What does verse 6 tell you to do? _____

List five specific ways that you can acknowledge Him:

1. _____
2. _____
3. _____
4. _____
5. _____

What will God do if you trust Him with all your heart, lean not on your own understanding, and acknowledge Him in all your ways? _____
_____
_____

The Lord will direct your paths. He will guide you, help you make decisions and keep you walking in His will. The Bible contains many more verses on trusting God. For your personal study, read Psalm 9:10; 13:5–6; 20:7; 22:4; 25; 31:5–6; 37:3–11; 56:3–4; 62:8; 91 and Isaiah 26:3.

A Heart of Unbelief

Worry and fear can be the result of a heart of unbelief. Hear me out, because I don't mean "unbelief" as in an unbeliever. I am referring to a believer that fails to take God at His word. Let's consider a few examples.

The first example concerns the sufficiency of God's grace. "And He said to me, 'My grace is sufficient for you, for My strength is made perfect in weakness'" (2 Cor. 12:9). Do you honestly believe God's grace is sufficient for you? How is that belief evidenced in your life? _____

_____

_____

God also promises to care for you. In Psalm 55:22 what does God promise to do if you cast your cares on Him? _____

_____

What does it mean to you that God will sustain you? _____

_____

_____

Being a Christian doesn't mean your life will always go smoothly. God will sustain you, but that does not mean that you will always get what you want, be on top of the world or be thrilled with your circumstances. It *does* mean that God will *always* give you the grace necessary so that you may glorify Him at any given moment. When you don't know what else to do, ask God what you should do at the moment to bring glory to His name. Many times the answer quietly comes back to worship Him.

Another example of God's support comes at the end of Psalm 55:22: "He will never let the righteous fall" (NIV). If you knew beyond the shadow of a doubt that your circumstances would never overwhelm you and that you would never fall apart, would you be at peace? _____

_____

A final example concerns the message of hope in Jeremiah 29:11–14:

> For I know the thoughts that I think toward you, says the LORD, thoughts of peace and not of evil, to give you a future and a hope. Then you will call upon Me and go and pray to Me, and I will listen to you. And you will seek Me and find Me, when you search for Me with all your heart. I will be found by you, says the LORD, and I will bring you back from your captivity; I will gather you from all the nations and from all the places where I have driven you, says the LORD, and I will bring you to the place from which I cause you to be carried away captive.

Do you believe that you have hope and a future? (The real question is—do you believe God or not?) How does this change your perspective on your current situation? _____

_____

_____

Living to Please Yourself Instead of Living to Please God

Anxiety can be the result of a life lived for self rather than for God. Worry, anxiety and fear, when you really think about it, are our response to viewing life through the lens of *what will this do to me*? How will this circumstance affect my life?

Do this little exercise: Make a list of the things you worry about. Ask God what it is about each issue that is the real cause of your worry and write that down as well.

I worry about . . .	My greatest fear about that is . . .
Ex. My husband spending his paycheck on alcohol	Ex. We won't be able to pay our bills, and we'll lose our house.

How many of the items that cause you to worry involve negative things that might happen to you?

_____

The only thing powerful enough to demolish fear at its very roots is God's perfect love (1 John 4:18). Note the contrast between God's way (love) and our way (fear)[7]:

God's Way (Love)	Man's Way (Fear)
Love looks for opportunities to give. (John 3:16; 1 John 3:16–18)	Fear keeps a wary eye on possible consequences of involvement.
Love lays down its life for others. (1 John 3:16)	Fear will not take personal risks to help another.
Love believes all things. (1 Cor. 13:7)	Fear is highly suspicious.

God's Way (Love)	Man's Way (Fear)
Love never fails. (1 Cor. 13:8)	Fear occasions greater fear; failure to assume responsibilities brings more fear of the consequences of acting irresponsibly.

Sometimes our fear is rooted in trying to protect ourselves from personal suffering. As such, it can be an extreme form of self-protection. Remember that life is not about you; it is about the sovereign Creator of the universe. That thought tends to put life in perspective.

Take a moment to write any questions you have or perhaps things that were unclear in this chapter:

_____

_____

_____

_____

There is one more exercise that can really help when your mind is on a run-away freight train and there seems to be no stopping it. These four questions will help you work from emotions to truth. Journal your responses.

1. What is the reality of my situation? What are my present (literal, physical) surroundings? (Worry tends to take you to another place and time in your thinking. Answering this question helps bring you back to the present.)

2. How can I give glory to God at this very moment?

3. Who does Jesus say I am? (Review in your mind as many things you can remember about who you are in Jesus Christ.[8])

4. What evidence is there right now that I have been to the cross? In other words, what evidence is there that my old self was crucified at the cross and that I have risen in newness of life? "I have been crucified with Christ; it is no longer I who live" (Gal. 2:20).

Worry, anxiety and fear are emotionally and physically draining, and they are unproductive. Ultimately, they are a manifestation of what we really believe about ourselves and about God. Pray to accept His all-sufficience!

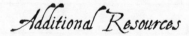

Additional Resources

Overcoming Fear, Worry and Anxiety by Elyse Fitzpatrick

Praying God's Word by Beth Moore

Self-Confrontation—A Manual for In-Depth Discipleship by The Biblical Counseling Foundation

Running Scared: Fear, Worry and the God of Rest by Dr. Edward T. Welch

Thinking Biblically about Worry by Paul Tripp, www.ligonier.org

Crossing the Jordan: Living Victoriously in Difficult Relationships

Application Questions

1. What one or two statements impacted me from this chapter?

    a. _____

    b. _____

2. How can I apply it/them to my life today and begin to pursue positive growth? _____

    _____

3. What one step am I willing to take to move toward heart change in my reactions, behavior or attitude? _____

    _____

4. What do I learn about God from this chapter? _____

    _____

5. How does His Word (the Bible) confirm this? _____

    _____

    _____

The "S Word": Submission

by Betsy Shoppy

Humble yourselves in the sight of the Lord, and He will lift you up.
James 4:10

10

"Submission" has become a dirty word in our society. The concept of submission is grossly misunderstood by men and women, believer and unbeliever alike, and it is an extremely emotional issue. For many years women's liberation advocates in America have fought not just for equality but often for superiority; much of that movement flies in the face of God and directly contradicts His truth and His divine design. Submission is God's idea—not man's and not your husband's. God had a wonderful design and plan in mind when He "created man in His own image; in the image of God He created him; male and female He created them" (Gen. 1:27). God did not leave us to guess how submission is to work; rather, He wrote it down for us in His instruction manual, the Bible.

As we begin our search through God's Word to see what He says on this subject, please understand that we do not take this topic lightly. We have prayerfully gathered this information and prepared this study deeply aware of the unique aspects of a home and marriage struggling with addiction.

Take a moment to ask God to open and prepare your heart to hear what *He* has for you in this area.

Growing in the area of submission requires the power of the Holy Spirit, because in the flesh we want our own way. Selfish attitudes prevent submission.[1] How many times have you thought or overheard someone say, "I am going to do my own thing my own way, and no one is going to tell me what I must do!" "I am my own boss!" In today's society this type of thinking is very prevalent. It has infiltrated our culture, crept into our thoughts and determined our actions. This way of thinking is sinful; it is the sin of self-centeredness, and it blinds us to the truth. Submission opposes that line of thinking. What comes to mind when you hear the word "submission?" How would you describe it? _____

_____

_____

Webster's Dictionary defines "submission": "to yield; resign; or surrender to power, or the will or authority of another individual."[2] *Vine's Expository Dictionary of New Testament Words* says it means "to rank under, to obey, to submit, or yield."[3] *Roget's Thesaurus* gives these synonyms for the verb "submit": "to yield, to acquiesce, to comply, to surrender, to obey."[4]

Submission, as God designed it, begins as an act of the will to transform the attitude of your mind and heart, which results in positive, God-honoring action. Anthony Gibson writes, "The road to freedom is through surrender."[5] It sounds paradoxical, but it isn't; in order to truly be "free," we must submit to Christ in every area of our lives. Choosing obedience, we leave the results to Him.

Our perfect example of a submissive spirit is that of Jesus Christ. Facing His arrest and crucifixion, Jesus cried out to His Father, "Father, if it is Your will, take this cup away from Me; nevertheless not

My will, but Yours, be done" (Luke 22:42). Please note that Jesus preferred not to have to suffer in this way ("take this cup away from Me"); yet He, by an act of His will, chose to surrender, or to put His will under the will of the Father ("nevertheless, not My will, but Yours, be done").

We are called to have the same mindset as Jesus Christ—being humble, submissive and obedient. "Let this mind be in you which was also in Christ Jesus, who, being in the form of God, did not consider it robbery to be equal with God, but made Himself of no reputation, taking the form of a bondservant, and coming in the likeness of men. And being found in appearance as a man, He humbled Himself and became obedient to the point of death, even the death of the cross. Therefore God also has highly exalted Him and given Him the name which is above every name, that at the name of Jesus every knee should bow, of those in heaven, and of those on earth, and of those under the earth, and that every tongue should confess that Jesus Christ is Lord, to the glory of God the Father." (Phil. 2:5–11).

Jesus was equal with God, yet He chose to submit His will to that of His Father. Did Jesus' choice make Him less God? No! Did His choice make Him less than the Father? No! But was it easy? No way! Jesus was beaten, humiliated, stripped, mocked, spit on, disbelieved and nailed to a cross. Yet not once did Christ accuse His betrayer (Judas) or retaliate against His tormentors. He did not blame them for the wrong they did or the suffering He endured, nor did He try to defend Himself. Why? Because He was steadfast in His obedience to His Father.

Peter depicts this beautiful picture of Christ's humble submission. "For to this you were called, because Christ also suffered for us, leaving us an example, that you should follow His steps: 'Who committed no sin, Nor was deceit found in His mouth'; who, when He was reviled, did not revile in return; when He suffered, He did not threaten, but committed Himself to Him who judges righteously" (1 Pet. 2:21–23).

You see, submission requires humility; you must choose to bring your will under the will of another. To submit your will to that of your husband requires that you die to yourself and that you do it out of a heartfelt desire to submit to God's will, looking past the circumstances and person to understand God's call. There is freedom under God's authority. You can trust Him to do what is best—even when you don't understand or when you disagree. Trust that He knows all things (past, present and future) and that you do not.

God's design for submission begins with your realization that He has absolute authority in your life and that He has ordained an authority structure in which "submission" must operate to be successful, one in which the wife can have protection and provision.

If your husband does not protect and provide for you does that let you off the hook? _____

_____

If yes, what biblical evidence can you provide? _____

_____

_____

_____

Elisabeth Elliot, Bible teacher and women's speaker, writes, "Submission is the recognition of authority that is divinely assigned."[6] "Let every soul be subject to the governing authorities. For there is no authority except from God, and the authorities that exist are appointed by God" (Rom. 13:1).

God has ordained an authority structure beginning with His sovereignty (His absolute control of and power over all things). The Godhead consists of the Father, the Son and the Holy Spirit, and the ultimate authority in this triune relationship is God Himself. The word sovereign depicts the idea of God's supreme authority. Ephesians 1:11 says that God "works all things according to the counsel of His will." The very first verse of the Bible, Genesis 1:1, says, "In the beginning God created the heavens and the earth." God the Creator is in absolute control over all creation.

Submission to God is key. If you do not first and foremost submit to God, you will be unable to submit to the other, lesser authorities in your life in a way that is glorifying to God. As God's children, we are to humbly and obediently accept our place in His order. Let's search the Scriptures to see God's ordained structure in five areas: the church, the family, the government, the workplace and society.

Authority Structures

The Church

The local church is a group of believers that regularly worship and learn together. Each biblical local church has an internal structure of authority, which God has ordained and within which every believer lives.

"Shepherd the flock of God which is among you, serving as overseers, not by compulsion but willingly, not for dishonest gain but eagerly; nor as being lords over those entrusted to you, but being examples to the flock . . . Likewise you younger people, submit yourselves to your elders" (1 Pet. 5:2–3, 5).

Are you a member of a local, Bible-believing New Testament church? _____
If yes, does your church practice biblical church discipline? _____
_____
_____

Are you under the authority of that church? _____ If yes, what does that mean to you? _____
_____
_____

What is the responsibility that God gives to elders/deacons in First Peter 5:2? _____
_____
_____
_____

How are they to carry out this responsibility in everyday life? _____
_____
_____

Family: Wife to Husband, Husband to Christ, Children to Parents

The Scriptures clearly describe what the authority structure in the family should look like.

Wives and Husbands: "Wives, submit to your own husbands, as to the Lord. For the husband is head of the wife, as also Christ is head of the church; and He is the Savior of the body. Therefore, just as the church is subject to Christ, so let the wives be to their own husbands in everything. . . . Nevertheless let each one of you in particular so love his own wife as himself, and let the wife see that she respects her husband" (Eph. 5:22–24, 33).

"Wives, submit to your own husbands, as is fitting in the Lord" (Col. 3:18).

"Wives, likewise, be submissive to your own husbands, that even if some do not obey the word, they, without a word, may be won by the conduct of their wives, when they observe your chaste conduct accompanied by fear. Do not let your adornment be merely outward—arranging the hair, wearing gold, or putting on fine apparel— rather let it be the hidden person of the heart, with the incorruptible beauty of a gentle and quiet spirit, which is very precious in the sight of God" (1 Pet. 3:1–4).

(We'll expound more on the husband/wife relationship further on in the chapter.)

Children: "Children, obey your parents in the Lord, for this is right" (Eph. 6:1).

Government

Submission to the governing authorities may at times seem contrary to our faith or personal political leanings, but we must take God's Word as our guide.

"Let every soul be subject to the governing authorities. For there is no authority except from God, and the authorities that exist are appointed by God. Therefore whoever resists the authority resists the ordinance of God, and those who resist will bring judgment on themselves" (Rom. 13:1–2).

"Remind them to be subject to rulers and authorities, to obey, to be ready for every good work" (Titus 3:1).

"Therefore submit yourselves to every ordinance of man for the Lord's sake, whether to the king as supreme, or to governors, as to those who are sent by him for the punishment of evildoers and for the praise of those who do good. For this is the will of God, that by doing good you may put to silence the ignorance of foolish men—as free, yet not using liberty as a cloak for vice, but as bondservants of God. Honor all people. Love the brotherhood. Fear God. Honor the king" (1 Pet. 2:13–17).

Employers ("Masters")

The authority structure in the workplace has broken down in so many ways because of a failure to live according to God's ordained plan. Many want to do their own thing and refuse to submit to the organizational authorities designated by God.

"Bondservants, be obedient to those who are your masters according to the flesh, with fear and trembling, in sincerity of heart, as to Christ; not with eyeservice, as men-pleasers, but as bondservants of Christ, doing the will of God from the heart, with goodwill doing service, as to the Lord, and not to men, knowing that whatever good anyone does, he will receive the same from the Lord, whether he is a slave or free" (Eph. 6:5–8).

Society

How we live in community with one another matters to God. He speaks of it in His word.

". . . submitting to one another in the fear of God" (Eph. 5:21).

"Yes, all of you *be submissive to one another*, and be clothed with humility, for 'God resists the proud, but gives grace to the humble'" (1 Pet. 5:5).

Read First Peter 5:5. What does it command the younger men/women to do? _____
_____

Point to ponder: "Often the real proof of our obedience is the willingness to submit, not only to adversity, but also to the specific individuals whom God has placed over us."[7]

What do the above verses say to you regarding the principle of submission? _____
_____
_____
_____

What did the Lord Jesus say to the Father regarding His death on the cross in Luke 22:42, and what lessons can we learn from this verse? _____
_____
_____
_____
_____

It's often said that no man is an island. We do not function in isolation; we function as a body. As part of the body of Christ, we live in community. We are called to love our brethren (1 John 4:21), and part of loving them involves exhorting them to live holy and godly lives. "Brethren, if a man is overtaken in any trespass, you who are spiritual restore such a one in a spirit of gentleness, considering yourself lest you also be tempted. Bear one another's burdens, and so fulfill the law of Christ" (Gal. 6:1–2).

Rev. Tim Shorey, speaking at a couples' weekend at America's Keswick, defined biblical accountability as, "Taking responsibility for duties placed on my life. Being responsible to people, to answer to someone, and submitting to those in authority. It involves recognition of God's authority structures and submitting willingly to the conviction, correction and consequences when habitual sins are committed. It is connectedness with correction and consequences."[8] Accountability is somewhat foreign to the world, and although it is biblical, it is often unfamiliar even within the church, yet it is God's ordained structure to facilitate our growth and safety.

The Family Structure

Another vital part of God's authority structure is the family. It is central to the human race. It is one He created and ordained, and it is highly emphasized in Scripture. God views the family with great love and concern.

In their book *Embrace the Serpent*, Marilyn Quayle and her sister, Nancy Northcott, included the following dedication: "Family is the wellspring from which flows faith, integrity, compassion, confidence, industry, selflessness, spirit—the strength of the soul and the basis of national strength. When family fails, the nation fails."[9]

In Genesis 2:18 and 4:1–2, we see how God regarded Adam's singleness. "And the LORD GOD said, 'It is not good that man should be alone; I will make him a helper comparable to him'" (Gen. 2:18). "Now Adam knew Eve his wife, and she conceived and bore Cain, and said, 'I have acquired a man from the LORD.' Then she bore again, this time his brother Abel" (Gen. 4:1–2). See the emphasis God placed on beginning a family. What was Eve's response in 4:1? _____

_____

_____

Family relationships are also in God's ordained line of authority. Let's consider the husband and wife relationship and what God's Word says in this area. Remember Jesus' example—His submission did not make Him less or lower than the Father. In the same way, your choice to surrender and to submit your will does not make you less or lower than your husband. God gave both the husband and wife individual and vital responsibilities.

Let us first consider the husband's role. Ephesians 5:25–29 says,

> Husbands, love your wives, just as Christ also loved the church and gave Himself for her, that He might sanctify and cleanse her with the washing of water by the word, that He might present her to Himself a glorious church, not having spot or wrinkle or any such thing, but that she should be holy and without blemish. So husbands ought to love their own wives as their own bodies; he who loves his wife loves himself. For no one ever hated his own flesh, but nourishes and cherishes it, just as the Lord does the church.

How is the husband to love his wife? _____

_____

_____

What are your thoughts about this kind of love? _____

_____

_____

_____

The word for "love" used in Ephesians 5:25, as well as in Colossians 3:19 ("Husbands, *love* your wives and do not be bitter toward them"), is *agape*, which is Greek for "to love and keep on loving." To whom is this command specifically addressed? _____

This sounds wonderful doesn't it? *If only it was really like this*, we think. But wait a minute! If we want our husbands to obey this Scripture and love us, we too have to obey Scripture and submit to them. It is as difficult for our husbands to biblically love us as it is for us to biblically submit to them.

Colossians 3:19 both gives the command to love and admonishes husbands not to be sharp, cutting and harsh, but rather to be tender and gentle and to build up their wives. Aside from providing growth in the home by reading God's Word to the family, the husband must also treasure and treat his wife tenderly. Now you may be thinking, *but he doesn't treasure me OR treat me very tenderly*. Did Judas's disobedience negate the necessity of Christ's obedience? No. Neither does your husband's disobedience negate the necessity of your obedience. "The 'agape' word for love in the above verses means, as previously stated, to keep on loving, love sacrificially and never let your love grow cold. It includes emotions and actions. It chooses to care deeply. It never fails and it guards against unforgivingness and apathy."[10]

Wives should help and complete their husbands, but this is not always an easy task. Consider these hindrances to submission: bitterness, disrespect, disloyalty, fear, anger, extended family, mistrust and hatred.

What others can you think of or do you personally struggle with? _____
_____
_____

Regardless of our struggles, God's design and desire for us as wives is to be submissive, and He speaks clearly and plainly on this issue. In her book *By Design*, Susan Hunt beautifully describes biblical submission "as the wife having an attitude of joyful and willing submission to the God-ordained authority and protection of her husband."[11]

First Peter 3:1–4 gives us further instruction on how to behave as wives: "Wives, likewise, be submissive to your own husbands, that even if some do not obey the word, they, without a word, may be won by the conduct of their wives, when they observe your chaste conduct accompanied by fear . . . rather let it be the hidden person of the heart, with the incorruptible beauty of a gentle and quiet spirit, which is very precious in the sight of God" (3:1–2, 4). What are the principles from this verse for us to follow?
_____
_____

Is there anything causing you to live in a contrary way to this verse? If so, what and why? _____
_____
_____
_____

Ask God to help you specifically in that area.

Peter says that our spirits should be "gentle and quiet." "Gentle" involves having a heart that accepts God's dealings as good and for our welfare. "Quiet" involves having a heart settled in tranquility and deep peace, and peace is a gift the Lord freely offers us: "Peace I leave with you, My peace I give to you; not as the world gives do I give to you" (John 14:27).

Let's consider some additional verses of Scripture that speak of wives' submission. Colossians 3:18 tells wives to be subject to their own husbands "as is fitting in the Lord." In Ephesians 5:22 God says to wives, "submit to your own husbands, as to the Lord." This is not a one-time act but a continual submission; it's a choice and an act of the will. Do you desire to have the godly habit to be biblically submissive? Then take note of this: "Every habit grows out of a succession of little acts. No habit comes full-grown into your life; it grows like the roots of a tree, like the rivers of the flesh, as the morsels of food are absorbed into your body."[12] We must nurture an attitude of submission, because this attitude will lead to proper actions and reactions.

It is the Christian wife's duty to submit to her husband in the Lord's design. "For the husband is head of the wife, as also Christ is head of the church; and He is the Savior of the body. Therefore, just as the church is subject to Christ, so let the wives be to their own husbands in everything" (Eph. 5:23–24). When you face difficult times, look beyond your husband and look to the Lord, knowing you are being obedient to Him; submit "as to the Lord."

Remember that submission has much more to do with your relationship with God than it does with your relationship with your husband. Godly submission requires more trust in a loving heavenly Father who cares for you than trust in your husband. You may experience negative consequences because of unwise choices your husband makes, but God is still in control. God may use unwise choices and the resulting consequences to convict your husband of sin and/or to develop a certain Christ-like character quality in him. You do not want your unwillingness and your unyielding spirit to hinder God's work in your life and your husband's.

Now, there are some exceptions to the command for wives to be subject to their husbands. These include immoral acts, illegal decisions and situations that threaten the life of the wife or children. The husband/wife relationship is never meant to be totally controlled or dominated by the husband; there should be dialogue on all relationship issues.

Examples of areas that should be discussed between husband and wife include family decisions, finances, child rearing (discipline) and spiritual leadership (the husband should assume his responsibility to lead, and his wife should encourage—not nag—him). If after much discussion and prayer, differences of opinion between husband and wife over a certain problem remain, the wife should submit to her husband's leadership. Submission is not about being quiet, although sometimes it may call for that; rather, it is having a loving attitude, a willing heart, a graceful way of expressing opinions and an accepting spirit—even when we disagree with our husbands.

What issues do you have difficulty discussing with your husband? _____
_____
_____

Take these issues to the Lord and ask Him to give you wisdom and to help you talk to your husband about them. So what do you do when you're locked in battle of wills—when what you want is different from what he wants? We mentioned earlier about the necessity of dying to self in order to be successful in submission. How do you do that? A.B. Simpson beautifully addresses this in his book *The Christ Life*, not specifically regarding a wife's submission but rather surrender to God's will: "Only when we cease from our manly or womanly strength and become dependent can we know His strength as our support and stay." Further, "How may we, the believer, maintain this abiding life? You have surrendered; you have given up your strength as well as your will; you have consented that henceforth He shall support your life. Like a true bride, you have given up your very person, your name, your independence, so that now He is to be your Lord, Your very life is merged in Him, and He becomes your Head and your All in All."[13]

How can you surrender in light of your trying circumstances? It is a moment-by-moment act of your will—and God will give you the grace for each moment.

> Learn this secret, that you are not sanctified for all time so that there will be no more need for grace and victory, but you have grace for this moment, and the next, and by the time life is spent, you shall have had a whole ocean of His grace . . . Next, this abiding must be established by a succession of definite acts of will, and of real, fixed, steadfast trust in Christ . . . It does not come as a spontaneous and ir-resistible impulse that carries you whether you will or not, but you have to begin by an act of trust, and you must repeat it until it becomes a habit . . . If we would abide in Christ we must continually study to have no confidence in self.[14]

"Nevertheless let each one of you in particular so love his own wife as himself, and let the wife see that she respects her husband" (Eph. 5:33). This verse tells the wife to _____ her husband. Note that God adds no qualifications to this command.

Rewrite Ephesians 5:33 in your own words, inserting your name and your husband's: _____
_____
_____
_____
_____
_____
_____

Submission may seem humanly overwhelming, but with the enabling power, direction and guidance of the Holy Spirit, we can obey God's command. Wives who are born-again believers with Jesus Christ as their Savior, have the advantage of the Holy Spirit—the "Helper" (John 14:16, 26; 15:26; 16:7–8). The Greek word for "Helper" is *Paraklete*, which carries the connotations of advising, exhorting, com-forting, strengthening and encouraging. This *Paraklete* lives within you when you're born-again and is there waiting to give you all you need in the area of marital submission.

In summary, while God gives us wives the weighty command to submit to our husbands, He also pro-vides the resources for us to submit. With obedience and submission come blessings.

Take some time to write down situations when you have faced difficulties in your marriage—yet have submitted and been blessed. Consider asking others for examples of their own victories in this area as it can be an encouragement. _____
_____
_____
_____

As you pray over this area in your life, read and study these verses for encouragement:

- ❖ Psalm 37
- ❖ Psalm 107
- ❖ Isaiah 45:2
- ❖ Matthew 11:28–30
- ❖ John 14:16–17, 27
- ❖ Romans 8:26–28, 31–39
- ❖ Romans 11:33–36
- ❖ Second Corinthians 2:14
- ❖ Second Corinthians 10:4–5
- ❖ Second Corinthians 12:9
- ❖ Ephesians 3:12
- ❖ Philippians 4:13,19
- ❖ First Peter 5:7–8
- ❖ John 1:9

Additional Resources

All the Women of the Bible by Herbert Lockyer

Celebration of Womanhood by Miriam Bundy

True Women by Design; Spiritual Mothering; Leadership of Women in the Local Church

by Susan Hunt

The Excellent Wife by Martha Peace

Praying God's Word by Beth Moore

Recovering Biblical Manhood & Womanhood by John Piper and Wayne Grudem

Application Questions

1. What one or two statements impacted me from this chapter?

   a. _____

   b. _____

2. How can I apply it/them to my life today and begin to pursue positive growth? _____

   _____

3. What one step am I willing to take to move toward heart change in my reactions, behavior or attitude? _____

   _____

4. What do I learn about God from this chapter? _____

   _____

5. How does His Word (the Bible) confirm this? _____

   _____

   _____

u

The "R Word" : Respect

by Diane Hunt

Let the wife see that she respects and reverences her husband [that she notices him, regards him, honors him, prefers him, venerates, and esteems him; and that she defers to him, praises him, and loves and admires him exceedingly.]

Ephesians 5:33 (AMP)

*T*ruth be told, many of us struggle with issues of respect. Would you consider yourself disrespectful? (You may want to hold your answer until you've worked through this chapter.)

Addiction complicates issues of respect, but in my experience as a counselor, being respectful is a pervasive struggle for many, if not most, wives. "Respect" is a word most of us have eliminated from our vocabulary when it comes to our husbands. I'd like to share a little of my own journey in this area.

A few years ago, the mother of my daughter's friend told him that she disliked how disrespectfully I spoke to my husband and asked if my daughter did the same thing to him. I was mortified, hurt and angry—but even if I did not agree with the mode or method she used, I knew immediately that she was right. I took a good, hard look at my attitude toward my husband and realized I had a sinful habit of making harsh side comments, "mocking" him with sarcasm, laughing at him, correcting him, belittling him, etc.; I said it was all in good fun, but I knew better.

At the time this came to my attention, my behavior was probably at its all-time worst. I repeatedly dishonored my husband, and to make matters worse, I did it in front of my children. I watched as they also disrespected my husband. What could I say to them? I knew they were following my example. As a result of the other mother's interaction with my daughter, I made the choice to stop disrespecting my husband. At that point I did not put on active respect; I only purposed to stop the active disrespect.

A few years passed. Then early one December morning, I was listening to author and speaker Dr. Eggerichs talk about respect on the radio, and I was challenged to go the next step—to actively put on respect. My marriage has never been the same. I have put forth this same challenge to a number of other wives, and *without exception*, each has reported a positive change in her relationship. I want to remind you that our goal is holiness. Our goal is obedience to Jesus Christ, and respecting our husbands is part of that. Our goal is to live *coram Deo*—before the face of God—in a way that is pleasing to Him.

Let me give another illustration; if you have children, grandchildren, nieces or nephews, you will probably quickly identify with this one. Two teenagers, a brother and a sister, are sitting watching television. Mom, noticing that the dinner dishes are still on the table and that the kitchen has yet to be put in order, comes downstairs and finds the two staring at the set. Knowing it is her son's turn to be on kitchen duty, Mom reminds him of his chore: "Tom, it's your night to clean up; please get up and do it." His response? "But Mom, Susie didn't do it yesterday, and she still hasn't swept the floor. How come you never get on *her* case?"

What do you think most moms would say to his argument? _____
_____
_____

My response would have been, "Tom, your obedience has nothing to do with your sister. I will deal with her. You need to focus on doing what you are asked to do, regardless of your sister's obedience or lack of obedience." Are you with me? Why do our children think that just because their siblings aren't doing what is right that it somehow lets them off the hook? We need to stress the importance of their obedience, regardless of exterior circumstances, and pray that they eventually understand.

We may be surprised by our children's attitudes, yet adults come into my counseling office all the time exhibiting the same mind-set. They somehow believe that if their spouses are not behaving correctly, they do not need to do what is right either. Be honest—have you ever thought this way?

Have you ever used another's behavior to justify your disobedience to God's Word? If so, how? _____
_____
_____

How do you view the role of the Word of God in your daily choices, attitudes and behaviors? _____
_____
_____

Take time to really ponder that question before you proceed. Let me encourage you to pray your way through this chapter. Ask God to give you a pliable heart that He can shape in His hands. Ask Him to open your eyes to His truth and for the power and courage to obey what He shows you. Take a moment to express your thoughts in a prayer. _____
_____
_____
_____
_____

Respect can't be earned, because if it was, it would mean our husband's negative behavior would prohibit us from obeying God, and no person can come between you and your heavenly Father. Regardless of what your husband does, daily commit to live out your biblical role in the power of the Holy Spirit. This is one of those commands in God's Word that, in our flesh, we often justify away, ignoring our responsibility to respect because our husband is not doing what he is supposed to be doing. But remember—just because something is difficult doesn't mean we aren't expected to obey God or that He'll cut us a break.

Your obedience to God's Word is not all about you. You must come to the place where you "understand that your marriage is not primarily about you and your spouse but that it's about you and Jesus Christ. Marriage is a test of how you unconditionally love and respect your spouse as you obey, honor and please the Lord. Primarily, you don't practice love and respect to meet your needs in your marriage, as important as these are. Your first goal is to obey and please Christ . . . your first goal is to obey and please the Lord."[1]

Proclaim, "I will sacrificially serve my husband today. I will love and respect him as if he were Christ Himself." Dr. Eggerichs highlights this principle: "No matter how depressing or irritating my spouse might be, my response is my responsibility."[2] This is freeing. You can *choose* to do right. You can *choose* to obey and please Jesus Christ even when your spouse does not—and you will be blessed for your obedience even if your spouse never changes.

Please do not misunderstand; I am not encouraging you to enable your husband in sinful behavior. I am also not encouraging you to lie down to be walked over like a doormat. The discernment required to know when to submit and when to speak requires a very close walk with Jesus Christ and a reliance on the guidance of the Holy Spirit: "I will instruct you and teach you in the way you should go; I will guide you with My eye" (Ps. 32:8).

Read Ephesians 5:33. According to the verse, what two things is God clearly commanding and to whom is He commanding it? _____

_____

_____

_____

We want to use a megaphone to repeat and point out the Scripture that says, "Let each one of you in particular so love his own wife as himself," and slip the part that says, "Let the wife see that she respects her husband" under the couch cushion with last night's forgotten popcorn kernels, but this verse exhorts us to respect our husbands. While you may be prone to emphasize your husband's love over your respect, both are equally important for a flourishing and God-glorifying relationship.

According to MarriageToday founder Dr. Evans, the roles specified in Ephesians 5 are designed by God to neutralize our sinful natures and to keep them from destroying our marriages.[3] Evans says that, generally speaking, a woman's "sin nature" is prideful independence. For example, Eve didn't ask for her husband's input before eating from the tree in the Garden of Eden even though he was with her (Gen 3:6). And, generally speaking, a man's sin nature is passive insensitivity. To follow the previous example, note that Adam did not stop Eve from talking to the serpent or eating the fruit, and he unquestioningly ate the fruit Eve gave him.

According to Genesis 3, what were the lures Satan used to tempt Eve? _____

_____

_____

_____

I hope one of the things you wrote was that she saw that the tree was able to make her wise. In verse 5 Satan told her, "For God knows that in the day you eat of it your eyes will be opened, and you will be like God, knowing good and evil." Ultimately, Eve's willingness to disobey in order to obtain wisdom revealed her heart to be independent from God and perhaps her husband. She wanted to be *like* God instead of *dependent* on God.

The Purpose of Marriage Roles

Let's return to Ephesians 5:33. Evans says the God-ordained roles in this verse are specifically intended to:

1) Disarm our sinful natures. Consider:

- In the flesh women are prone to prideful independence, so what does God call them to do? To be submissive, honorable and respectful.
- In the flesh men are prone to passive insensitivity, so what does God call them to do? To be servant leaders.[3]

No one gets an easier job; it is as difficult for men to be servants and leaders as it is for women to be respectfully submissive. Both require the supernatural power of the Holy Spirit! Submission, honor and respect are not things our husbands earn; rather they are attributes that characterize who we are. Our actions and words are born out of what we are.

Can you be characterized as a woman of submission, honor and respect? Why or why not? _____

_____

_____

2) Foster heart-to-heart intimacy with our spouses. Consider:

- Neither a man who feels dishonored or disrespected nor a woman who feels unloved will desire to be intimate (and I don't mean just sex) with his/her spouse on a heart-to-heart level.[4] Ever wonder why your husband doesn't seem to open up to you or share his heart with you? Is it possible he doesn't feeling respected?

The number one desire of a man is honor. Men often have big egos, and women tend to sneer at them. But what if "ego" is just a man-made term that describes a sensitive part of man's personality, intentionally designed by God? Aren't you equally as sensitive in areas such as appearance, emotions and relationships?

Think about it—if your husband surrounded you with a warm sense of total security, absolute trust, abundant admiration and effusive love, would you not be more likely to draw near to him and open your heart? Likewise, when your husband feels your honor and respect for him and when he is confident of your admiration for him as a man, he will be more prone to trust you and to open his heart to you.

Living Respectfully

Every morning before your feet hit the floor, offer up a prayer committing yourself to live the entire day to God's glory (1 Cor. 10:31). Choose to live today as a woman of honor and respect, no matter what! Your heart will be blessed by your obedience, and your relationship with your spouse will deepen.

Do you believe that respect is something in our character which controls what we do? Why or why not?

_____

_____

_____

Let's face it—your husband has behaved and will behave in ways that defy respect. You may say, "I'll respect my husband when he's doing what's right, but surely I don't have to respect him when he is sinning." Wrong. You should not ignore his sinful behavior, but your approach to him should always reflect your character—respect, honor and dignity.

Write 1 Peter 3:1–2: _____

_____

_____

_____

Take another look at verse 1; it tells us husbands can be "won by the conduct of their wives" even if they "[do] not obey the word." That's huge! Other translations use such phrases as "any (that) are disobedient to the word" (NASB) and so "that if any of them do not believe the word" (NIV). Here's a great paraphrase from *The Message*:

> The same goes for you wives: Be good wives to your husbands, responsive to their needs.

> There are husbands who, indifferent as they are to any words about God, will be captivated by your life of holy beauty. What matters is not your outer appearance—the styling of your hair, the jewelry you wear, the cut of your clothes—but your inner disposition. (1 Pet. 3: 1–4)

I like the part about our husbands being captivated by our lives of *holy beauty*. What does this mean to you? What kind of inner disposition do you think you reveal to your husband? _____

_____

_____

Two main points to remember:

1. We are called to respect and submit to our husbands—even when they aren't obeying the Word and even if they aren't believers. So even if you don't like his choice, unless it is unlawful or sinful, respectfully submit.

2. Prayers will get us much further than nagging words. The sooner we learn that and alter our behavior accordingly, the sooner we will be on our way to a closer, God-honoring marriage.

According to Evans, biblical love involves "A permanent, self-sacrificing commitment to act in the best interest of another person regardless of negative emotions or difficult circumstances."[5] Love and respect are acts of the will.

There are times when we don't act very lovable, yet we would be upset if our husband said or even thought to himself, "She is not acting lovable right now, so I am not going to love her; she needs to earn my love." Yet we turn around and use that same logic in saying we'll ignore our husbands or treat them with disrespect until they earn our respect by acting correctly. That is an unfair double standard!

Is any of this hitting home for you? In what ways have you believed or acted like your husband must earn your respect? _____
_____
_____
_____

Being respectful—no matter what the circumstances—is humanly impossible. Apart from the Holy Spirit living out this truth through us, we will not succeed. There have been times when I have pursed my lips to keep from apologizing for dishonoring my husband, but thankfully the Holy Spirit prevailed, and I sought my husband's forgiveness.

It was extremely difficult for me when the Lord brought me under conviction about my lack of respect. It frequently felt extremely unnatural to submit, serve and respect, but as months and months have passed, it has gotten easier. I have seen the fruit of my progress, and it is well worth the effort.

Examples of Disrespectful Women

Of course, I'm not the only woman who has struggled with being respectful. Let's take a look at a few examples of disrespectful women from the Bible.

Michal: Saul's daughter and King David's wife. Please read Second Samuel 6:12–23, and answer the following questions.

Why was David dancing before the Lord with all his might? _____
_____
_____

What was Michal's response when she saw David out the window? _____
_____
_____

When David came home, what was he intending to do? _____
_____
_____

Describe the manner in which Michal addressed David upon his return: _____
_____
_____

How would you characterize David's response to her? _____
_____

Ultimately, what consequence did Michal have to live with as a result of this interaction? _____
_____
_____

You may ask why I think her barrenness was a result of this interaction. Study the first word in verse 23; "therefore" indicates "as a result of what came before," or "what follows is a consequence." I don't know if God prevented Michal from becoming pregnant or if David so withdrew from her that they did not have sex and thereby prevented conception, but either way, Michal suffered a negative consequence for her actions.

Delilah: Samson's wife. Let's face it—no one needs a wife like Delilah. Samson must have been a little slow on the uptake considering the numerous times he told her his secret knowing full well (after the first time) that she was setting him up. Please read Judges 16: 4–22 and answer the following questions.

What ploy did Delilah use to try to get Samson to tell her the truth? (16:15) _____

_____

What did she do daily with her words, and what do we call that today? _____

_____

_____

How did it affect Samson? _____

_____

_____

What did Delilah's nagging lead to? _____

_____

_____

Scripture calls a nagging woman contentious. Proverbs 19:13 tells us, "And the contentions of a wife are a continual dripping," and 27:15–16 echoes, "A continual dripping on a very rainy day and a contentious woman are alike; whoever restrains her restrains the wind, and grasps oil with his right hand." In these verses nagging sounds akin to Chinese water torture. Do you really want to be thought of as a nag?

The reality is we nag to get our way; we want something done or changed, and when we don't see it happening, we nag. Ladies, we have all done it. I jokingly tell my husband that if he would just do what I tell him to do the first time, I wouldn't have to nag. I am slowly learning to pause and take my own counsel in this area.

Here is a good rule of thumb: Communicate your heart to your husband in a manner that you are sure he will hear—once. That's right, *once*. If he brings it up again, feel free to discuss it respectfully and openly. If he does not, pray. Every communication you have about that matter from that point on should be between you and God. Pray until God changes your husband's heart or yours. Tommy Nelson, in *The Book of Romance*, writes, "All of us are under authority of someone, and in the marriage chain of command, a husband is under the authority of God. A wife is wise to trust God to manifest His authority in her husband's life rather than to attempt to take on that role for herself."[6] I would encourage you to beseech God to exercise His authority in your husband's life, because He has power that you do not. Only God can change your husband's heart. I know that goes down hard, but the sooner you and I get on board with God's plan and His chain-of-command rather than our own, the sooner we can live all-out for Jesus Christ.

Another interesting study in the Scriptures of a woman who dishonored her husband is **Rebekah**. Her story is in Genesis 27:1–28:9. The consequence of her siding with her son Jacob against her husband, Isaac, was strife between her sons, Jacob and Esau, to the point that Esau vowed to kill Jacob. We have to ask ourselves, "How is my disrespect of my husband affecting my children?"

If you have children or if others (including strangers) have witnessed your disrespectful behavior, how do you think it affected them? _____

_____

Write Hebrews 12:14–15: _____

_____

_____

_____

Do you see how your bitter attitude of disrespect can poison not only you but also those around you?

Examples of Respectful Women

Let's move on from the negative examples to the positive. There are several, but for our purposes we will focus on three, Abigail, Esther and Sarah.

Abigail: Nabal's wife, then King David's wife. Abigail's husband, Nabal, foolishly turned away the king's men. Abigail, hearing of this offense, acted quickly to protect her family and appease the king. Let's look at her approach to King David. Read First Samuel 25:1–44.

What posture did Abigail take before David? (25:23) _____

_____

I am not suggesting you bow down at your husband's feet, but I am suggesting you exhibit the attitude Abigail's gesture indicated. What attitude did she portray? _____

_____

You will notice that Abigail seeks to affirm David in her approach (25:26–31). What are some of the things she said to him? _____

_____

_____

I want to make note of a very important concept; there is wisdom in carefully choosing your timing in your approach to your husband:

Now Abigail went to Nabal, and there he was, holding a feast in his house, like the feast of a king. *And Nabal's heart was merry within him, for he was very drunk; therefore she told him nothing, little or much, until morning light.* So it was, in the morning, when the wine had gone from Nabal, and his wife had told him these things, that his heart died within him, and he became like a stone. (25: 36–37)

See how Abigail "told him nothing until daybreak." When Nabal was sober, "his wife told him all things." Wanting to confront your husband when he is drunk or high is understandable but foolish. Choose your timing prayerfully. Have you ever confronted your husband when he was in an altered state of mind? You probably didn't get very far. Earlier on I shared the principle that you should share your heart once in a way that your husband will be most likely to hear; when he is drunk or high is not that time. Flee instead to the arms of your heavenly Husband, Jesus Christ, and pour your heart out to Him. Wait to speak to your husband until he is not under the influence or the aftereffects of his addiction.

Esther: Her story is found in the book of the Bible by her name—Esther. You should read the entire book, but for the purposes of our study, some excerpts will suffice.

Esther's story begins with Queen Vashti's refusal of her husband's request to come to a party. The king's advisors said,

> For the queen's behavior will become known to all women, so that they will despise their husbands in their eyes, when they report, 'King Ahasuerus commanded Queen Vashti to be brought in before him, but she did not come.' This very day the noble ladies of Persia and Media will say to all the king's officials that they have heard of the behavior of the queen. Thus there will be excessive contempt and wrath. (Esther 1:17–18)

Because of Vashti's disobedience, the king dethroned his queen and appointed commissioners to search his kingdom for a suitable replacement.

Esther was a Jewish girl brought up by her cousin, Mordecai, and she was one of the young women brought to the palace for the king's consideration. She greatly pleased King Ahasuerus: "The king loved Esther more than all the other women, and she obtained grace and favor in his sight more than all the virgins; so he set the royal crown upon her head and made her queen instead of Vashti" (2:17).

Esther's reign was not defined by light romance, however. Read Esther 3:8–15, keeping in mind that Haman was the king's right-hand man.

What did Haman seek to do, and how would this affect Esther? _____

_____

_____

Since Haman was intending to destroy the Jews, Mordecai sent word to Esther, "that he might command her to go in to the king to make supplication to him and plead before him for her people" (4:8). Esther's response to Mordecai was, "All the king's servants and the people of the king's provinces know that any man or woman who goes into the inner court to the king, who has not been called, he has but one law: put all to death, except the one to whom the king holds out the golden scepter, that he may live. Yet I myself have not been called to go in to the king these thirty days" (4:11). Mordecai answered, "Do not think in your heart that you will escape in the king's palace any more than all the other Jews. For if you remain completely silent at this time, relief and deliverance will arise for the Jews from another place, but you and your father's house will perish. Yet who knows whether you have come to the kingdom for such a time as this?" (4:12–14).

For such a time as this. Do you see the position of power and strength God put Esther in? Hers was by no means a passive role. Read Esther 4:15–16 to find out how she handled her peculiar position. What did she instruct Mordecai to do and what did she intend to do? _____

_____

_____

_____

In her statement, "If I perish, I perish," Esther expresses her heart to serve a cause greater than herself; she demonstrates an other-centered perspective.

Read Esther 5:1–2. When did Esther approach the king? _____

_____

Notice that Esther respected the rules of the kingdom. Esther 4:11 reminds us that a person who came before the king without being summoned would be put to death unless the king extended his gold scepter, so Esther waited for him to do that before she spoke.

Read Esther 5:4–7. What evidence do you see in these verses that Esther demonstrated respect to her husband, the king? Write as many as you can find. _____

_____

_____

_____

Read Esther 6:1–10. God has a sense of humor, don't you think? Haman ended up honoring the very one he wanted to disgrace. When you're dealing with a difficult issue with your husband, always remember that God is at work even when you can't see it.

Esther planned carefully, and she was patient to express her request at the appropriate time. I love the words of Esther in response to the king's question:

And on the second day, at the banquet of wine, the king again said to Esther, 'What is your petition, Queen Esther? It shall be granted you. And what is your request, up to half the kingdom? It shall be done!' Then Queen Esther answered and said, "If I have found favor in your sight, O king, and if it pleases the king, let my life be given me at my petition, and my people at my request. For we have been sold, my people and I, to be destroyed, to be killed, and to be annihilated. Had we been sold as male and female slaves, I would have held my tongue, although the enemy could never compensate for the king's loss. (7:2–4)

How would you characterize her words (use as many descriptive terms as possible)? _____

_____

_____

_____

I believe Esther is a good example of a woman of honor, respect and grace. She did not allow fear to prevent her from what she knew she was to do—for who knows but that she came to "royal position for such a time as this" (4:14, NIV). Have you considered that perhaps God has brought you to your specific husband and your specific family "for such a time as this"?

Sarah:

I don't plan to do an in-depth study of the life and marriage of Sarah; I just want us to consider a New Testament reference to her: "For in this manner, in former times, the holy women who trusted in God also adorned themselves, being submissive to their own husbands, as Sarah obeyed Abraham, calling him lord, whose daughters you are if you do good and are not afraid with any terror" (1 Pet. 3:5–6). Let's not get too bogged down with the obeyed and master part. What I want you to see is the very last sentence: "and do not give way to fear" (NIV).

I believe fear is often our excuse for failing to obey God in this area of respecting our husbands. Fear of loss, fear of being a doormat, fear of things never changing, fear of not being loved—the list could go on and on. Sarah was able to overcome her fears by placing her hope in God. You too can put your trust in God and not your husband, and you can choose to respect in spite of fear.

Let's look at a few more references in First Peter before closing with some practical applications.

Write First Peter 3:4: _____

_____

_____

Describe what a quiet and gentle spirit means to you: _____

_____

_____

Ask your husband what a quiet and gentle spirit is to him. Write his response here: _____

_____

_____

Notice that a quiet and gentle spirit is of great worth and is "very precious in the sight of God" (1 Pet. 3:4). Don't fall into the trap I did; I might have had a quiet spirit, but there was nothing gentle about it. I was quiet, but I was clenching my teeth and setting my jaw, and I don't think that is what God intends for us to do. We need to be both soft and loving. First Peter 3:9 challenges us to live by a high standard: "not returning evil for evil or reviling for reviling, but on the contrary blessing, knowing that you were called to this, that you may inherit a blessing."

In Summary

Okay, I know I've given you a lot of information to process, so let's wrap up with a practical how-to. How do we demonstrate active respect for our husbands?

1. **Repent.** Seek God's forgiveness for failing to obey His command to respect your husband.

2. **Pray.** Ask God to show you how you are currently disrespecting your husband. Ask God to give you creative ways to actively show respect to and for your husband in ways that he will understand.

3. **Ask for forgiveness** from your husband for failing in various ways to show him respect.

4. **Put off your disrespectful words and ways.** If you slip, seek forgiveness from God and from your husband.

5. **Put on active respect.** Respect is not passive; it's active. Demonstrate respect in your words, expressions and attitude—both to your husband and when talking about him to others. Be respectful in the way you look at him, and listen to him when he talks.[7]

Remember:

✧ As godly women we are to be characterized by our honor, dignity, respect and grace.

✧ God calls wives to respect their husbands unconditionally. In the same way you don't have to earn your husband's love, he doesn't have to earn your respect.

✧ Respect can be a two-part process. First, stop actively disrespecting your husband. Second, show active respect through word and deed.

✧ Our respect for our husbands is not about their behavior; it's about our character.

✧ Respect does not preclude speaking your opinion into a situation. A good rule of thumb is to tell you husband your concern once. Then, from that point on, pray.

✧ Fear can be a great inhibitor of respectful obedience. Choose to be respectful, no matter what, by placing your hope in God.

✧ Pray for the power of the Holy Spirit to be obedient.

Disrespect is everywhere you look. You can see it on television, in movies and in supermarkets. It has become more the norm than the exception. As followers of Jesus Christ, we can stand apart from the world by genuinely respecting our husbands.

I believe that God wants strong marriages that reflect His glory. He will empower our marriages, our homes and families. In so doing, He will rebuild our churches and our nation.

Additional Resources

Motivating Your Man God's Way by Dr. Emerson and Sarah Eggerichs

Love and Respect by Dr. Emerson Eggerichs

"How to Build Lasting Romance, Intimacy, and Sexual Pleasure in Your Marriage,"
CD Series by Jimmy Evans

Application Questions

1. What one or two statements impacted me from this chapter?

   a. _____

   b. _____

2. How can I apply it/them to my life today and begin to pursue positive growth? _____

   _____

3. What one step am I willing to take to move toward heart change in my reactions, behavior or attitude? _____

   _____

4. What do I learn about God from this chapter? _____

   _____

5. How does His Word (the Bible) confirm this? _____

   _____

   _____

Intimacy with God, Our Heavenly Husband

by Diane Hunt

*When You said, "Seek My face," my heart said to You, "Your face, L*ORD*, I will seek"*

Psalm 27:8

*W*omen long to love and to be loved, yet the more we try to demand love from our husbands, the more elusive it becomes. And the more we demand it and fail to receive it, the more discontented we become. You have probably heard the expression "looking for love in all the wrong places." The truth is that anyone or anything other than Christ that we look to for comfort, love or well-being draws us away from the One True Lover of our soul. This list can include our husbands, our children, our bank accounts, our homes, our friends, etc.

You see, all our needs for intimacy are met first and foremost in the Lord Jesus Christ. When we really see and live with Jesus as our heavenly Husband, our relational needs are met primarily in Christ, and the other pressures in our lives are reduced:

> For this reason I bow my knees to the Father of our Lord Jesus Christ, from whom the whole family in heaven and earth is named, that He would grant you, according to the riches of His glory, to be strengthened with might through His Spirit in the inner man, that Christ may dwell in your hearts through faith; that you, being rooted and grounded in love, may be able to comprehend with all the saints what is the width and length and depth and height—to know the love of Christ which passes knowledge; that you may be filled with all the fullness of God. (Eph. 3:14–19)

My whole life outlook changed when I discovered Christ as my heavenly Husband. Let me rewind; for a significant period of time, I was after my husband to develop heart-to-heart intimacy with me. I was frustrated, and he was befuddled. Then, one day when I was counseling, the Lord clearly spoke to my spirit as this thought penetrated my mind: "The intimacy you desire with your husband is what I want with you." This prompting of the Holy Spirit began my journey of pursuing intimacy with Christ.

Allow me to encourage you to likewise draw near to the Lord. "My soul, wait silently for God alone, for my expectation is from Him" (Ps. 62:5).When your perceived needs are met by your heavenly Husband, you will find contentment and satisfaction in Christ, and it will remove your desperate demands of love from your husband.

Have you ever noticed your false expectations getting you into trouble? What types of expectations cause you the most problems? _____
_____
_____

What is your typical response when your expectations as to how an evening, a visit, a family trip will go aren't met? How do you respond when things don't turn out the way you planned? _____

_____

_____

_____

_____

We are sure to be disappointed when we depend on people to meet our expectations. As Psalm 118:8–9 teaches, "It is better to trust in the LORD than to put confidence in man. It is better to trust in the LORD than to put confidence in princes."

Our society breeds discontentment; no matter what you have, there is always someone who has more. From finances to family histories, from belongings to relationships, there is always someone better off than we are. When we're discontent, we pursue more—either literally or emotionally. But this is not the life to which God has called us: "Not that I speak in regard to need, for I have learned in whatever state I am, to be content" (Phil. 4:11). When you pursue Christ as your heavenly Husband, you will be wholly satisfied in Him. As First Timothy 6:6 reminds us, "Now godliness with contentment is great gain."

Of course there will be times when we lack contentment because God has created a need in our lives that He wants to fill. Consider Adam:

> And the LORD God said, "It is not good that man should be alone; I will make a helper comparable to him." Out of the ground the LORD God formed every beast of the field and every bird of the air, and brought them to Adam to see what he would call them. And whatever Adam called each living creature, that was its name. So Adam gave names to all cattle, to the birds of the air, and to every beast of the field. But for Adam there was not found a helper comparable to him. And the LORD God caused a deep sleep to fall on Adam, and he slept; and He took one of his ribs, and closed up the flesh in its place. Then the rib which the LORD God had taken from man He made into a woman, and He brought her to the man. (Gen. 2:18–22).

From this text we can see that God made Adam aware of his need and then filled that need.

God creates the need so we will go to Him to have that need satisfied.

> For He satisfies the longing soul,
> And fills the hungry soul with goodness. (Ps. 107:9)

A parent's goal is to take a dependent baby and raise him/her to be independent. God's goal is just the opposite. He takes His independent children and raises them to dependence on Him.

Read Jeremiah 31:25 and John 10:10. What does it mean that the Lord will satiate/satisfy/refresh you?

_____

_____

_____

What expectations, needs or longings are you currently experiencing? _____

_____

_____

Whatever you're longing for is not necessarily wrong; in fact, most of our desires are God-given. The problem is that we desire them too much. We take a good thing and make it an idol, making that thing vital to our happiness and contentment.

When we are not satiated in Christ, truly satisfied in Him, we wander and look for satisfaction elsewhere, and this is the root of many of life's problems—including everything from addiction to loneliness. We look to others to have our relational needs met. If our contentment is dependent on others—our children's obedience, our parent's acceptance and approval, our husband's sobriety or his attention—we're in trouble. When we believe our needs should and will be met by others, we fail to look to God; but when we look to God to meet our longings, He will never disappoint us.

Our relational longings should and can only be filled by Christ. "O God, You are my God; early will I seek You; my soul thirsts for You, my flesh longs for You in a dry and weary land where there is no water" (Ps. 63:1).

What would it look like for you to be satiated in Jesus Christ—to have all your expectations, needs and longings met by Him? _____

_____

_____

_____

_____

If you want to do a really great study, work your way through the book of Psalms and record all the different ways your Groom is defined. Here is a very brief summary: Jesus is my Creator (Ps. 95:6), my Fortress/Tower (18:2), my Rock (92:15), my Lord/Master (16:2), my Redeemer (19:14), my Refuge (57:1), my Shelter (61:3–4), my Deliverer (34:4) (by the way, Deliverer was by far the most prevalent title in my study at forty-nine occurrences!), my Hope (71:5), my Sustainer (55:22) and my Glory (3:3). In the course of my studies, I discovered seventy-five truths about my Groom. If you are interested in finding more than I've given here, hit the Book yourself and search Him out.

Christ is everything to us. "For He Himself is our peace, who has made both one, and has broken down the middle wall of separation" (Eph. 2:14).

God is our Creator. We are His. "Know that the LORD, He is God; it is He who has made us, and not we ourselves; we are His people and the sheep of His pasture" (Ps. 100:3).

He keeps His Word. "My covenant I will not break, Nor alter the word that has gone out of My lips. Once I have sworn by My holiness; I will not lie to David" (Ps. 89:34–35).

There is pleasure and delight in His presence. "You will show me the path of life; in Your presence is fullness of joy; at Your right hand are pleasures forevermore" (Ps. 16:11).

He protects us. "You are my hiding place; You shall preserve me from trouble; You shall surround me with songs of deliverance. Selah" (Ps. 32:7).

God desires intimate relationship with us. "I will betroth you to Me forever; Yes, I will betroth you to Me in righteousness and justice, in lovingkindness and mercy; I will betroth you to Me in faithfulness, and you shall know the LORD" (Hos. 2:19–20).

He is our heavenly Husband. "For your Maker is your husband, The LORD of hosts is His name; and your Redeemer is the Holy One of Israel; He is called the God of the whole earth" (Isa. 54:5). XXX

He listens. "I cried to the LORD with my voice, and He heard me from His holy hill. Selah" (Ps. 3:4).

Your heavenly Husband will never interrupt you or roll His eyes. He'll never walk away in a huff. He listens with undivided attention at all times (something only God, even while orchestrating six billion people's lives, can do). He never takes His eyes off of you. Psalm 121:3–4 tells us, "He will not allow your foot to be moved; He who keeps you will not slumber. Behold, He who keeps Israel shall neither slumber nor sleep."

God knows the deepest places of our heart. "Would not God search this out? For He knows the secrets of the heart" (Ps. 44:21).

Knowing these truths is only the beginning. Growth and change happen when we make these truths our own. Charles Spurgeon, renowned preacher and author, says, "To take up a general truth and make it our own, by personal faith is the highest wisdom. It is but poor comfort to say, 'The Lord is a refuge,' but to say, 'He is my refuge', is the essence of consolation."[1]

What to you are the three most meaningful attributes of your Groom? Why are they the most meaningful? _____
_____
_____
_____
_____
_____
_____

What attribute do you struggle the most to accept and why? _____
_____
_____
_____

The Creator of the Universe wants fellowship with you, one of His creations.

"That which we have seen and heard we declare to you, that you also may have fellowship with us; and truly our fellowship is with the Father and with His Son Jesus Christ. And these things we write to you that your joy may be full" (1 John 1:3–4).

Let the thought sink in that God desires deep relationship with you. "God is faithful, by whom you were called into the fellowship of His Son, Jesus Christ our Lord" (1 Cor. 1:9).

In the booklet "My Heart—Christ's Home," which presents a wonderful analogy about opening every area of life to Christ, Christ is pictured as saying, "The trouble with you is this: You have been thinking of quiet time, of the Bible study and prayer time, as a factor in your own spiritual progress, but you have forgotten that this hour means something to Me also. Remember, I love you. I have redeemed you at a great cost. I desire your fellowship. Now, He said, do not neglect this hour if only for My sake.

Whatever else may be your desire, remember I want your fellowship."[2]

How does it make you feel that God wants fellowship with you? _____
_____
_____

Perhaps deep intimacy with Jesus is something you have never known or maybe you have but have strayed in more recent times. It is never too late to begin or begin again. "For the eyes of the LORD run to and fro throughout the whole earth, to show Himself strong on behalf of those whose heart is loyal to Him" (2 Chron. 16:9).

If you have been struggling in your relationship with Christ, you can have hope that change is possible. "Now may the God of hope fill you with all joy and peace as you trust in Him, so that you may overflow with hope by the power of the Holy Spirit" (Rom. 15:13, NIV).

So how do we grow in intimacy with Christ? "The secret lies not in ten steps, and not in approaching the Bible as a self-improvement guide, but in being deeply in love with Jesus, so that your desire is to be completely abandoned to Him and receive whatever He has for you. Those who learn to relate to Jesus as the Love of their life, on a moment by moment basis, have a vitality surpassing that of most believers and a freedom from sins that once imprisoned them."[3]

If, when all is said and done and this study is tucked neatly on your shelf, we have equipped you with tools for living but have failed to point you and lead you to the Person of Jesus Christ, we have failed. Period. Life to the full is only found in Him.

How Can We Develop Intimate Fellowship with Christ?

Repentance

The best place to begin is always with repentance and confession. Ask God to search your heart and reveal any sins that need to be confessed. Pray Psalm 139:23–24: "Search me, O God, and know my heart; try me, and know my anxieties; and see if there is any wicked way in me, and lead me in the way everlasting." This is an important first step because it will open up the avenue between you and God. Sin interferes with the openness between you and God. Psalm 66:18–19 says, "If I regard iniquity in my heart, the Lord will not hear. But certainly God has heard me; He has attended to the voice of my prayer." What do you need to repent of? Well, if you haven't had an intimate relationship with Christ or if you've looked elsewhere for the love only He can give, acknowledging and confessing that shortcoming is a good place to begin.

Prayer

Ask God to change you. You are a work in progress—a work that will not be complete until the day you see Him face to face. God has promised to conform every single believer into the image of His Son, Jesus. "But we all, with unveiled face, beholding as in a mirror the glory of the Lord, are being transformed into the same image from glory to glory, just as by the Spirit of the Lord" (2 Cor. 3:18). As one of His children, He longs to make you like Jesus. Do you desire the same?

In our human nature we are more inclined to love ourselves than to love God. *Ask God to give you a passionate heart to love Him.*

Ask God to make you wholehearted toward Him. "Jesus said to him, '"You shall love the LORD your God with all your heart, with all your soul, and with all your mind." This is the first and great commandment'" (Matt. 22:37–38).

Do you long for the Lord as a parched tongue yearns for water? "As the deer pants for the water brooks, so pants my soul for You, O God. My soul thirsts . . . for the living God" (Ps. 42:1–2).

Notice the verbs the psalmist uses: longs, faints and cries out. He is yearning for God. Are you? "My soul longs, yes, even faints for the courts of the LORD; my heart and my flesh cry out for the living God" (Ps. 84:1–2).

Ask God to make you know the depth of His love for you. Even if we know of God's love in our heads, many of us do not feel it or believe it from our hearts. When we really understand the magnitude of His love not just for the world but for us as individuals, we are forever changed. "Though the mountains be shaken and the hills be removed, yet my unfailing love for you will not be shaken nor my covenant of peace be removed, says the LORD, who has compassion on you" (Isa. 54:10, NIV).

Oh, that we would know the width, length, depth and height of His love. "For this reason I bow my knees to the Father of our Lord Jesus Christ, from whom the whole family in heaven and earth is named, that He would grant you, according to the riches of His glory, to be strengthened with might through His Spirit in the inner man, that Christ may dwell in your hearts through faith; that you, being rooted and grounded in love, may be able to comprehend with all the saints what is the width and length and depth and height—to know the love of Christ which passes knowledge; that you may be filled with all the fullness of God" (Eph. 3:14–19). You do not simply need to know *about* Christ; you need to truly *know Him*. Do you see it? "To know the love of Christ which passes knowledge." Knowing the love of Christ results in being filled with all the fullness of God. Wow, sign me up! What does this verse from Ephesians mean to you personally? _____

_____

_____

_____

Behold Him

Synonyms for behold: "regard, gaze upon, view; watch; discern."[4] In order to behold Christ:

We need to know Him as a personal God. "God is a person, and in the deep of His mighty nature He thinks, wills, enjoys, feels, loves, desires, and suffers as any other person may. . . . Being made in His image we have within us the capacity to know Him."[5] Psalm 46:10 states, "Be still, and know that I am God."

We need to praise and worship Him. As we engage our minds in active praise, prayer and worship—either in word or song—we consider Him. When you worship, engage your heart and mind and reverence the Lord. "Give me an undivided heart that I may fear your name" (Ps. 86:11, NIV). Practice in the quietness of your own home; this will make corporate worship more meaningful.

We need to meditate on Him. Mull over what you know about Christ. Contemplate Him, His attributes, His works and His promises. "As you sit there behold Him, look at Him. Don't try to be like Him, just look at Him. Just be occupied with Him. Forget about trying to be like Him. Instead of letting that fill our mind and heart, let Him fill it. Just behold Him, look upon Him through the Word."[6]

We need to abide in Him. To abide means to dwell, remain and last.

Look up the following verses: Psalm 91:1; John 8:31; John 15:7; John 15:10.

What insight do you gain from these texts about abiding in Christ? _____
_____
_____
_____
_____

Abiding requires obedience. You cannot expect to abide in Christ but live life on your own terms. "He who says he abides in Him ought himself also to walk just as He walked" (1 John 2:6).

Abiding goes two ways. Consider the following verses:

> By this we know that we abide in Him, and He in us, because He has given us of His Spirit. Whoever confesses that Jesus is the Son of God, God abides in him, and he in God. And we have known and believed the love that God has for us. God is love, and he who abides in love abides in God, and God in him. (1 John 4:13–16)

> Abide in Me, and I in you. As the branch cannot bear fruit of itself unless it abides in the vine, neither can you, unless you abide in Me. (John 15:4)

How would living out the truth of these verses affect your daily life? _____
_____
_____
_____
_____

As you abide in Christ, you will grow more and more intimate with your Savior, and you will be fully content in Him. Proverbs 19:23 says, "The fear of the LORD leads to life, and he who has it will abide in satisfaction."

Making It Real in Your Life

Remember when you first fell in love? Think back to that time. Do you remember your thoughts and behaviors? (If you can't remember that time for yourself, think about how a friend acted when she fell in love.)

When you truly love Jesus Christ and delight yourself in Him, you exhibit some of the same attitudes and behaviors. Remember, God is incorporeal (without a body), but He is a Person. He has a mind, a will and emotions just like we do (in fact, we got them from Him), though without sin. To get to know Him, you should do many of the same things you would do with any person:

Hang onto His Every Word

In his commentary on Psalm 119 in *The Treasury of David*, Charles Spurgeon writes, "Heart-fellowship with God is enjoyed through a love of the Word, which is God's way of communicating with the soul by His Spirit."[7]

God's Word enables us to know Him, not just about Him. "It is not mere words that nourish the soul, but God Himself, and unless and until the hearers find God in personal experience they are not the better for having heard the truth. The Bible is not an end in itself, but a means to bring men to an intimate and satisfying knowledge of God, that they may enter into Him, that they may delight in His Presence, may taste and know the inner sweetness of the very God Himself in the core and center of their hearts."[8]

What does it look like to delight in God's presence? Psalm 119 includes 176 verses of the author expressing his pleasure in God. Here are a few excerpts:

"My soul breaks with longing for Your judgments at all times" (119:20).

"Your testimonies also are my delight and my counselors" (119:24).

"Unless Your law had been my delight, I would then have perished in my affliction" (119:92).

"How sweet are Your words to my taste, sweeter than honey to my mouth!" (119:103).

Spend time in the Word, reading, studying, researching and memorizing it. Immerse yourself in it. If you are not already reading Scripture daily, make a commitment to begin with just ten minutes a day. Most likely that ten minutes will become twenty minutes and then thirty as you delight in spending time with your Groom. Everyone can find ten minutes a day to do something that is important to them. Is this important enough to you to add this practice to your daily routine?

Expect Him to Do Husbandly Things

Author and speaker Anabel Gillham states, "Your relationship is only as real as you allow it to be."[9] Our heavenly Husband may not physically hug and kiss us, but I think we overlook a great deal that Jesus does to demonstrate His love for us—a beautiful sunset, a laughing baby, a twenty-dollar bill in the laundry, a great parking space, a gentle breeze on a warm day, etc. can all be reminders of His care. If we are not purposely looking for them, we will miss them.

What "hugs" have you gotten from God recently? _____
_____
_____
_____
_____

How have you responded? Perhaps you have responded by saying "Thank You, Lord." Have you ever considered responding "I love You too, Lord?"

Cry Out to Him

Intimacy develops as you realize you can go to God for *everything*. Pour out your heart to Him. He will hear you, and He will heal you. "O Lord, my God, I cried out to You, and You healed me" (Ps. 30:2).

In Psalm 94:19 the psalmist identifies God as His refuge: "In the multitude of my anxieties within me, Your comforts delight my soul."

God is our Comforter. What current burden are you carrying that you would like to cry out to Your heavenly Husband about? _____
_____

Tarry with Him

When you are in love, you enjoy being with the object of your love. How can you say you love God when you don't want to spend time with Him? Perhaps you say quick prayers asking for guidance and then race on your way without waiting for an answer; instead take time to tarry (delay, linger, stay for a time) with your Groom. When you need direction, go to God and wait until He answers.

Meditate on these verses for encouragement to wait:

"Wait on the LORD; be of good courage, and He shall strengthen your heart; wait, I say, on the LORD!" (Ps. 27:14).

"But those who wait on the LORD shall renew their strength; they shall mount up with wings like eagles, they shall run and not be weary, they shall walk and not faint" (Isa. 40:31).

"Show me Your ways, O LORD; teach me Your paths. Lead me in Your truth and teach me, for You are the God of my salvation; on you I wait all the day" (Ps. 25:4–5).

What do you find the hardest thing about tarrying with the Lord? _____
_____
_____

Share Your Excitement about Your Groom

Ever notice how people in love find a way to make every conversation about the one they love? When we are in love with Jesus, it is only natural for us to want to weave Him into our conversations, sharing our delight in Him. "Sing to Him, sing psalms to Him; talk of all His wondrous works!" (Ps. 105:2).

Wouldn't it be great if others wanted to know about Jesus because of your obvious delight in Him? When we have the sweet aroma of Christ, His presence is evident wherever we go. "Now thanks be to God who always leads us in triumph in Christ, and through us diffuses the fragrance of His knowledge in every place" (2 Cor. 2:14).

I know this has been a long chapter, and believe me I have just scratched the surface. I hope this study whetted your appetite to want to know more and to grow in your intimate relationship with Jesus Christ. As you long for and pursue deep intimate fellowship with Jesus Christ, your heavenly Husband, you will find rest for your soul and be fully satisfied in Him and Him alone.

Additional Resources

Falling in Love with Jesus by D. Brestin and K. Troccoli

The Confident Woman by Anabel Gillham

A Divine Invitation by Steve McVey

Principles of Spiritual Growth by Miles Stanford

The Pursuit of God by A.W. Tozer

Application Questions

1. What one or two statements impacted me from this chapter?

   a. _____

   b. _____

2. How can I apply it/them to my life today and begin to pursue positive growth? _____

   _____

3. What one step am I willing to take to move toward heart change in my reactions, behavior or attitude? _____

   _____

4. What do I learn about God from this chapter? _____

   _____

5. How does His Word (the Bible) confirm this? _____

   _____

   _____

13

Marital Intimacy

by Diane Hunt

For this reason a man will leave his father and mother and be united to his wife, and they will become one flesh.

Genesis 2:24, NIV

13

*I*t would have been easy to skirt the topic of sexual intimacy, but to keep with our commitment to deal with the tough issues, we press on. Sex has the potential to be a very controversial issue between a husband and wife, and throughout my years of counseling, I've heard a variety of comments from men and women regarding their attitudes toward sex. Issues of sexual intimacy are not unique to couples in which one or both are struggling with addiction; however, addiction presents additional emotional and sometimes physical hurdles to overcome.

I want to be extremely sensitive to the many facets of marital intimacy. Please try to set aside your emotions and opinions and give clear consideration to the Word of God. This chapter will address false intimacy, nonphysical intimacy, physical intimacy, hindrances to true intimacy and personal responsibility, and we'll conclude with some basic biblical principles in an effort to address frequently asked questions. While you are working through this chapter, you may have several "yeah, but . . ." questions; I think you will find many of them dealt with in the FAQ section.

One of my goals in writing this chapter is to elevate the nonphysical aspects of intimacy to the same level as the physical. I believe that one reason I have a regular stream of women in my office who want a valid reason not to have sex is because the emotional component, which is so vital to a well-functioning marriage, has been minimized. When emotions are overlooked, sex becomes a duty rather than a delight, and this can cause marital strain. (If this has never been a problem for you, then you would be in the minority among women I have counseled.)

Let's start our study on intimacy where the Bible starts. Please write out Genesis 2:24: _____
_____
_____

How do you understand the concept of leaving? _____
_____

How do you understand the concept of cleaving or being joined to your spouse? _____
_____

How have you done the "leaving?" _____
_____

How have you done the "cleaving?" _____
_____

True intimacy is only possible within the framework of a committed, honest relationship. Genesis 2:25 describes Adam and Eve living in total freedom with one another: "And they were both naked, the man and his wife, and were not ashamed."

Now, I believe one of the purposes of marriage is sex; it is not *the only* purpose, but it is one. True intimacy, however, involves more than sex. When a husband and wife are both actively building a positive relationship and seeking to be other-centered in their choices and actions, intimacy grows. And when nonphysical intimacy (emotional oneness) and physical intimacy (physical oneness) are balanced, the result is a beautiful, fulfilling relationship that brings much glory to God. When we make God's glory a higher priority in our lives than self-fulfillment or happiness, a great deal of pain, suffering and disappointment is avoided.

Do you agree with that statement or not? Why or why not? _____
_____

Let's consider some Scriptures to guide us as we proceed:

> You and your husband can glorify God together. "Now may the God of patience and comfort grant you to be like-minded toward one another, according to Christ Jesus, that you may with one mind and one mouth glorify the God and Father of our Lord Jesus Christ" (Rom. 15:5–6).

> We are called to be other-centered rather than self-centered. "Let no one seek his own, but each one the other's well-being" (1 Cor. 10:24). "Let nothing be done through selfish ambition or conceit, but in lowliness of mind let each esteem others better than himself. Let each of you look out not only for his own interests, but also for the interests of others" (Phil. 2:3–4).

Each of these verses speaks of the power of a mutually committed relationship. A solid marriage is a balance of both emotional and physical intimacy.

How do you define intimacy? _____
_____
_____

How do you think your husband would define intimacy? _____
_____
_____

How do these definitions differ? _____
_____
_____

False Intimacy

God delights in sexual oneness; within marriage sex brings glory to Him. It was His idea after all (see Gen. 2:24). Tim Gardner, in his book *Sacred Sex*, reminds us of "the privilege of entering into God's presence through the oneness of sex."[1]

That said, the Bible clearly states that sex is intended by God to be enjoyed *within the commitment of a marriage*—not before nor in addition to. Multiple Scriptures condemn extramarital relations:

> "For this you know, that no fornicator, unclean person, nor covetous man, who is an idolater, has any inheritance in the kingdom of Christ and God" (Eph. 5:5).

> "Marriage is honorable among all, and the bed undefiled; but fornicators and adulterers God will judge" (Heb. 13:4).

"Fornication" is defined as "consensual sexual intercourse between two persons not married to each other."[2] In my research I learned about how premarital sex actually prevents relational development:

> A couple's sexual relationship prior to marriage can easily create what I call 'artificial intimacy.' Artificial intimacy describes the sensation of closeness that is inherent in mutual sexual arousal. Our bodies feel good being close to one another. Often we equate that good feeling with trust and openness. Yet that sensation is deceptive because it can feel vulnerable, emotionally open, and trusting when it's not at all. . . . A couple may feel close when they're not close at all. Their intimacy is artificial—not real . . . A couple's relationship before marriage can be compared to a steam pipe that contains and transports pressure. The pipe has several small cracks that are invisible to the eye. At the end of the pipe is an exhaust valve that can be opened or closed. As long as the valve is open, the pressure is released and the cracks never emit any steam—they're never discovered and repaired. Eventually they'll corrode and destroy the pipe. Only when the valve remains closed so that pressure can build can the cracks be discovered and repaired.

> All couples have weak points—or cracks—in their communication patterns: different viewpoints, biases, sensitivities, family differences, role expectations. Since communication is the area of real intimacy, these cracks are important to discover. But if a couple is opening the exhaust valve of sex, normal pressure doesn't have the chance to build. Many communication flaws won't become evident until they are severe. And for many couples, that's too late.[3]

According to author Dr. Harry W. Schaumburg, false intimacy is "essentially a self-created illusion to help a person avoid the pain inherent in real intimacy."[4] Here's my definition: false intimacy is seeking the feelings of closeness and connectedness without the investment in relationship.

We can use sex to restore good feelings about our spouse and about our relationship, even when the underlying issue has not been resolved. In fact, "Sex can even be used to *avoid* intimacy."[5] How so?

> Sexually active couples often use the sensation of intimacy to deny the existence of conflict. A couple can go to bed, feel great about each other, and never resolve the real issue. Problems don't get resolved; they just get buried under artificial intimacy. The pattern can continue for a long time. The source of conflict often remains hidden, in fact, until unresolved tension develops into resentment.[6]

Resolving conflicts takes work. It requires openness, vulnerability, compromise and engagement—and sex is in no way an adequate substitute for real relationship. I've heard from professionals that men often gain a sense of comfort from sex; this might explain why they can have an argument at dinner and be ready for sex at nine. Their timing may not be good, but they are making an effort to reconnect. They want to know everything is okay.

You may be asking, "If my husband and I had an argument that hasn't been resolved, and I don't *feel* like having sex, should I?" Or, "What do I do if my husband wants sex and every cell of my body is screaming no?" Ephesians 4:26–27, says, "'Be angry and do not sin': do not let the sun go down on your wrath, nor give place to the devil." Realistically, you won't always be able to resolve every problem before bed; if this is the case, commit to discuss the issue at a specified time within the next day or two.

However, if you see a pattern of using sex to avoid intimacy, it is important to discuss this with your husband. Work to resolve any conflicts you are having, which will result in relational intimacy; this often results in the desire for sexual intimacy. Also, take time to pray. Ask God to give you a right heart and a warm desire for your husband; then step out in faith and trust God to bless your obedience. Pray and ask God to convict your husband if his motives are wrong or if he is seeking to avoid real intimacy; it is not helpful to guess at his intentions.

Another issue certainly worth mentioning is the propensity of some women to use sex as a tool of manipulation. This is not pleasing to God and must be confessed and repented of. If we consider that in every situation we can either minister or manipulate, as women of God, let's choose to minister.

The foundations for true intimacy are in Christ. First Corinthians 6:13–20 tells us,

> Now the body is not for sexual immorality but for the Lord, and the Lord for the body. And God both raised up the Lord and will also raise us up by His power. Do you not know that your bodies are members of Christ? Shall I then take the members of Christ and make them members of a harlot? Certainly not! Or do you not know that he who is joined to a harlot is one body with her? For "the two," He says, "shall become one flesh." But he who is joined to the Lord is one spirit with Him. Flee sexual immorality. Every sin that a man does is outside the body, but he who commits sexual immorality sins against his own body. Or do you not know that your body is the temple of the Holy Spirit who is in you, whom you have from God, and you are not your own? For you were bought at a price; therefore glorify God in your body and in your spirit, which are God's.

In other words, your body is not your own. There is something beautiful and holy about a person fully devoted to Christ—body, soul and spirit. Flee immorality in all its forms in order to glorify God and to protect your marriage and yourself. The Lord is just and quick to forgive if you have already been sexually active outside marriage, but choose to commit to keep your body pure from this date forward.

Write out Second Corinthians 7:1: _____

_____

_____

_____

False intimacy is combatted by true intimacy, which requires a life of purity and faithful commitment to God first and your husband second. In addition to sexual purity and commitment, God-glorifying marriages have a balance of nonphysical and physical intimacy.

Nonphysical or Emotional Intimacy

For a relationship that is God-glorifying and mutually fulfilling, nonphysical intimacy is just as vital as physical intimacy. (We'll speak later about how you can foster an environment that can nourish this exciting balance.) True intimacy is a result of oneness in relationship. It is a balance of emotional, spiritual and physical aspects. When emphasis is consistently put on one aspect to the detriment of another, we stray from God's intended design. I think Tim Gardner gets it right when he writes, "By inviting your mate inside your mind, your heart and your spirit, you're working to create the wholeness of oneness that gives sex its meaning and, ultimately, it's true pleasure."[7] In many situations emotional openness requires taking a risk, especially if you have allowed yourself to be vulnerable in the past only to be hurt. The risk requires that you trust God with your heart.

Let's think through Gardner's quote. How can you invite your mate inside your mind? _____
_____
_____
_____

How can you invite your mate inside your heart? _____
_____
_____

How can you invite your mate inside your spirit? _____
_____
_____

Read the following Scriptures and record the thoughts you glean as they relate to your marriage.

"When a man has taken a new wife, he shall not go out to war or be charged with any business; he shall be free at home one year, and bring happiness to his wife whom he has taken" (Deut. 24:5).

"Let your fountain be blessed, and rejoice with the wife of your youth" (Prov. 5:18).

"She does him good and not evil all the days of her life" (Prov. 31:12).

". . . submitting to one another in the fear of God" (Eph. 5:21).

"Wives, submit to your own husbands, as to the Lord . . . Husbands, love your wives, just as Christ also loved the church and gave Himself for her" (Eph. 5:22, 25).

"Husbands, likewise, dwell with them with understanding, giving honor to the wife, as to the weaker vessel, and as being heirs together of the grace of life, that your prayers may not be hindered" (1 Pet. 3:7).

_____
_____
_____
_____
_____
_____
_____
_____

Physical Intimacy

For those of you who skipped directly to this section, let me start by saying this is not a how-to manual. (Look at the additional resources list for books on this topic, such as *Intended for Pleasure* by Dr. Ed

Wheat.) Physical intimacy is a very important component in marriage, and it has potential to be a volatile area for couples with or without addiction in the mix.

I think the reason there is so much confusion and conflict with regard to sex is because culturally, both outside and inside the church, sex is spoken of in terms of "drive." It is defined as: "a physiological state corresponding to a strong need or desire."[8] Speaking of sex as a drive implies that the person is compelled beyond his/her self-control. Yet Scripture clearly indicates we can control ourselves: "For this is the will of God, your sanctification: that you should abstain from sexual immorality; that each of you should know how to possess his own vessel in sanctification and honor" (1 Thess. 4:3–4). We are not compelled to act in a way that is beyond our sanctified ability to control.

Physical and nonphysical intimacy are two different but related components of relationship. Sex is a physical act; it is something you do. Nonphysical intimacy is different; it's not so black and white, and men are typically uncomfortable in the emotional realm. Several men have told me that when they don't understand emotions, they often ignore them. It is not intentional; it just doesn't occur to them to think of the emotional component. It is the blend of physical and nonphysical intimacy that brings delight to both spouses. "Sex for sex's sake is not very appealing to a woman. But sex as the natural outcome of relational intimacy is very appealing."[9]

First Corinthians 7 is a controversial section of Scripture, but I believe it well depicts the necessary balance.

> Let the husband render to his wife the affection due her, and likewise also the wife to her husband. The wife does not have authority over her own body, but the husband does. And likewise the husband does not have authority over his own body, but the wife does. Do not deprive one another except with consent for a time, that you may give yourselves to fasting and prayer; and come together again so that Satan does not tempt you because of your lack of self control. But I say this as a concession, not as a commandment . . . But I say to the unmarried and to the widows: It is good for them if they remain even as I am; but if they cannot exercise self-control, let them marry. For it is better to marry than to burn with passion. (1 Cor. 7:3–9)

"Let the husband render to his wife the affection due her" does not necessarily mean sex. God designed men and women differently, and it is His intention that both husband and wife find fulfillment in marriage. God clearly indicates that sex is only for married couples because the parameters for a meaningful sex life are within a marital relationship. It is not a piece of paper saying you are married that makes your sex life pleasing to God; it is the loving relationship in which it is expressed.

That said, this verse from First Corinthians has been used far too often to make women feel guilty and ungodly when they struggle with having sex with their husband; it has been used to say that when a husband wants sex, it is his wife's duty to engage in it. Period. So what is your marital duty? Well, you and your husband are to be mutually pleasing to each other. You are to enjoy each other. And in a loving, caring, open, sharing relationship, sex will commonly be a natural way of expressing your love one for another. When sex becomes a duty, a responsibility or an item on your to-do list, something is off-kilter in the relationship. If this is the case for you, here are some possibilities as to what is amiss:

Attitude

God intended sex to be a mutually enjoyable experience. I'm chuckling as I recall an old Christian book I saw a while back of a "godly" woman's counsel on preparing a young woman to fulfill her marital duty. I can't remember all of it, but the gist was that sex is one of those things a woman just needs to grin and bear. How sad! A counselor asked a woman what she believed the purpose for sex was. This was her response: "I don't know if I'm sure what I believe. Obviously, it's to have children and it's something that men need, but beyond that I don't know. Right now I can take it or leave it." Perhaps you or your spouse have a wrong idea about God's delight in and design for sex. This could hinder a balanced, enjoyable sex life.

History

Perhaps you have experienced abuse or some other evil use of sex. You are not alone. You can be free from your past's controlling power over your present. Gardner writes,

> Sex has this same potential for good and bad. Sex provides the hope for good far beyond what most people dream or imagine. It can provide physical pleasure to be sure, but it is also a way of communicating tenderness, compassion, caring, and love. It is a way of showing our most intimate connection with our mates and a way of showing God's intimate communion with us. But untold millions have also been devastated and even destroyed, either emotionally, or physically, through the evils of sex. This evil that is associated with sex comes from the abuse of God's gift, not from the gift itself. God intended sex to be loving and pleasurable, not a source of heartache and destruction.[10]

Common questions related to this area of past abuses are: What if I am fearful? What if I just don't enjoy it? What if it makes me feel dirty? If you have been abused in the past and your sex life with your husband is being affected, seek help; find a good, professional, biblical counselor.

Isolation

Author and speaker Dennis Rainey writes, "Isolation is the number one problem in marriage relationships today."[11] Isolation can involve physical separation or simply refusing to talk, withholding affection, refusing to make eye contact, etc. Oneness, the opposite of isolation, is a balance between emotional, physical and spiritual aspects. If any one of these is ignored or overly emphasized, the relationship will be out of balance.

Expectations

Perhaps you or your husband have unreasonable expectations of romance/sex due to locker room talk, magazines, television, prior experiences, romance novels (it doesn't work like that), pornography (it doesn't work like that either), etc. I've heard it said that "reality can never measure up to fantasy." If you are being disappointed time and again, you need to take a look at what your expectations are and where you are getting them from. Consider Psalm 62:5: "My soul, wait silently for God alone, for my expectation is from Him."

Unresolved Conflict

Conflict happens. When conflict is left unresolved it will inevitably negatively impact the relationship and hinder intimacy. Make every effort to resolve conflict in a timely manner. "Therefore if you bring your gift to the altar, and there remember that your brother has something against you, leave your gift there before the altar, and go your way. First be reconciled to your brother, and then come and offer your gift" (Matt. 5:23–24).

Failing to Function within God-given Roles

God has ordained roles within the family. Ignoring or refusing to function within those guidelines is disobedient and may even be rebellious; either way will hinder your relationship with God and your spouse. Ephesians 5:22–33 tells us:

> Wives, submit to your own husbands, as to the Lord. For the husband is head of the wife, as also Christ is head of the church; and He is the Savior of the body. Therefore, just as the church is subject to Christ, so let the wives be to their own husbands in everything. Husbands, love your wives, just as Christ also loved the church and gave Himself for her, that He might sanctify and cleanse her with the washing of water by the word, that He might present her to Himself a glorious church, not having spot or wrinkle or any such thing, but that she should be holy and without blemish. So husbands ought to love their own wives as their own bodies; he who loves his wife loves himself. For no one ever hated his own flesh, but nourishes and cherishes it, just as the Lord does the church. For we are members of His body, of His flesh and of His bones. "For this reason a man shall leave his father and mother and be joined to his wife, and the two shall become one flesh." This is a great mystery, but I speak concerning Christ and the church. Nevertheless let each one of you in particular so love his own wife as himself and let the wife see that she respects her husband.

What other hindrances to intimacy can you think of? _____
_____
_____

If you're honest, which of these struggles are present in your relationship? (The answer to this is between you and God, and your husband if you choose to share.) _____
_____
_____
_____

Christian women have had it drilled into their heads that their marital duty is to submit to sex no matter what, but the God of the Bible wants our relationships to be a beautiful balance between emotional oneness and physical oneness. He is perfect love, gentleness and kindness. When a couple is fulfilling their God-ordained roles in marriage, the environment in the home is one of mutual love and respect, which fosters an emotional intimacy that naturally leads to physical intimacy. How can you do your part to create an environment in which mutual fulfillment can occur?
_____
_____
_____
_____
_____
_____

Reread First Corinthians 7:4–6, remembering that we cannot consider this verse in isolation apart from the whole counsel of God. ("For I have not shunned to declare to you the whole counsel of God," Acts 20:27.)

Personal Responsibility

Some time ago I read two excellent books on sexual or relational sin. The first was *Every Man's Battle* and the second *Every Woman's Battle*. It was my reading of these books that started me thinking about men's and women's specific struggles and responsibilities.

God designed men to be visually aroused. Their initial quickening of sexual arousal is not necessarily sin unless they intentionally seek it out, as in the case of pornography. Men can have a physiological sexual response that is completely out of their control. How they choose to react, however, is in their control. "I have made a covenant with my eyes; why then should I look upon a young woman?" (Job 31:1). Men not only need to avert their eyes but to avert their minds too. One of the authors of the book *Every Man's Battle* wrote that when he began to starve his eyes from finding pleasure in women other than his wife, she started to look better and better. When he refused to let his eyes wander, he was more satisfied by his wife.[12]

In much the same way as a man gains satisfaction from looking at women, women gain satisfaction from emotional connections. Most wives would not go so far as to physically get involved with another man, but they may enjoy his attention. In so doing they rob their spouses of their full devotion. Godly women must starve all outside interests, distractions and attention, and commit to being fully satisfied by their husbands.

I know this is extremely difficult when your spouse is not "there" for you emotionally, but keep in mind that your husband's behavior is never an excuse for you to disobey God. Choose to be pure; the more difficult it is, the more grace God will give you. "No temptation has overtaken you except such as is common to man; but God is faithful, who will not allow you to be tempted beyond what you are able, but with the temptation will also make the way of escape, that you may be able to bear it" (1 Cor. 10:13).

Purity is a matter of choice. Song of Solomon commands, "I charge you, O daughters of Jerusalem, by the gazelles or by the does of the field, do not stir up nor awaken love until it pleases" (2:7). This call to purity is lifelong; choosing to devote yourself to an upright lifestyle is just as vital after marriage as before.

There are specific things we can do to keep our bodies and minds in check. "But I discipline my body and bring it into subjection, lest, when I have preached to others, I myself should become disqualified" (1 Cor. 9:27).

If we allow ourselves to gain pleasure outside of our marriage, we will reap the negative consequences of such behavior. ("Do not be deceived, God is not mocked; for whatever a man sows, that he will also reap. For he who sows to his flesh will of the flesh reap corruption, but he who sows to the Spirit will of the Spirit reap everlasting life," Gal. 6:7–8.) The more we practice subtle behaviors that rob our spouse of what is his, the more justified we will feel and the more "natural" it will become for us to compromise our mental and physical purity. "For this is the will of God, your sanctification: that you should abstain from sexual immorality; that each of you should know how to possess his own vessel in sanctification and honor" (1 Thess. 4:3–4).

Write out Second Timothy 2:22: _____

_____

_____

_____

What is God impressing upon you to flee from? _____

_____

What positive attitudes and behaviors can you strengthen? _____

_____

Every individual is personally responsible to maintain a life of purity in body, mind and spirit, regardless of the choices others around them make. You get to choose to live life to glorify God above all else.

Principles of a Godly Life

Before we get to what I believe are some very common questions, I think it would be good to review some basic biblical principles that should frame our Christian lives and guide our thinking. I am no expert, and I don't have answers to all your questions, but the Lord does know all the answers, and He gives wisdom generously. ("If any of you lacks wisdom, let him ask of God, who gives to all liberally and without reproach, and it will be given to him," James 1:5.) Take a moment to pray for God to give you wisdom as you read this section.

What are some key scriptural truths for how we should handle relationships?

Pray

Every aspect of our lives should be bathed in prayer. "Let us therefore come boldly to the throne of grace, that we may obtain mercy and find grace to help in time of need" (Heb. 4:16).

Be Gentle, Kind and Respectful

"Therefore, as the elect of God, holy and beloved, put on tender mercies, kindness, humility, meekness, longsuffering; bearing with one another, and forgiving one another, if anyone has a complaint against another; even as Christ forgave you, so you also must do. But above all these things put on love, which is the bond of perfection" (Col. 3:12–14).

Be a Woman of Integrity and Dignity

"Wives, likewise, be submissive to your own husbands, that even if some do not obey the word, they, without a word, may be won by the conduct of their wives, when they observe your chaste conduct accompanied by fear. Do not let your adornment be merely outward—arranging the hair, wearing gold, or putting on fine apparel—rather let it be the hidden person of the heart, with the incorruptible beauty of a gentle and quiet spirit, which is very precious in the sight of God" (1 Pet. 3:1–4).

Fulfill Your Higher Calling

"Not that I have already attained, or am already perfected; but I press on, that I may lay hold of that for which Christ Jesus has also laid hold of me. . . . I press toward the goal for the prize of the upward call of God in Christ Jesus" (Phil. 3:12, 14).

"And whatever you do, do it heartily, as to the Lord and not to men, knowing that from the Lord you will receive the reward of the inheritance; for you serve the Lord Christ" (Col. 3:23–24).

Our obedience goes beyond submitting to our husbands; it goes directly to our willingness to submit to our Lord Jesus Christ. Rather than getting bogged down by your day-to-day struggles, take a moment to step back and remember the bigger picture. "If then you were raised with Christ, seek those things which are above, where Christ is, sitting at the right hand of God. Set your mind on things above, not on things on the earth. For you died, and your life is hidden with Christ in God" (Col. 3:1–3).

We live *coram Deo*, before the face of God. "To live coram Deo is to live one's entire life in the presence of God, under the authority of God, to the glory of God."[13]

Don't Whine or Complain

"Do all things without complaining and disputing, that you may become blameless and harmless, children of God without fault in the midst of a crooked and perverse generation, among whom you shine as lights in the world, holding fast the word of life, so that I may rejoice in the day of Christ that I have not run in vain or labored in vain" (Phil. 2:14–18).

What are you inclined to complain about? _____

_____

Consider Others before Yourself

"Let nothing be done through selfish ambition or conceit, but in lowliness of mind let each esteem others better than himself. Let each of you look out not only for his own interests, but also for the interests of others" (Phil. 2:3–4).

Use God's Guidelines to Discern Truth

"Who is wise and understanding among you? Let him show by good conduct that his works are done in the meekness of wisdom. But if you have bitter envy and self-seeking in your hearts, do not boast and lie against the truth. This wisdom does not descend from above, but is earthly, sensual, demonic. For where envy and self-seeking exist, confusion and every evil thing are there. But the wisdom that is from above is first pure, then peaceable, gentle, willing to yield, full of mercy and good fruits, without partiality and without hypocrisy. Now the fruit of righteousness is sown in peace by those who make peace" (James 3:13–18).

What are some very specific guidelines to discern if something is of heavenly wisdom? _____

_____

_____

Sow Seeds of Godly Attitudes and Behaviors

We reap what we sow. If we sow a discontented spirit, we will reap discontentment. If we sow anger, we reap bitterness. If we sow discord, we will reap strife and division.

"Do not be deceived, God is not mocked; for whatever a man sows, that he will also reap. For he who sows to his flesh will of the flesh reap corruption, but he who sows to the Spirit will of the Spirit reap everlasting life" (Gal. 6:7–8).

Err On the Side of Grace

"I desire mercy and not sacrifice" (Matt. 9:13).

I have made every effort to give you basics for your consideration regarding marital intimacy, but I'm sure you still have questions; the following section will hopefully answer some of them.

Frequently Asked Questions

I'm sorry to say there are not definitive biblical answers to every question concerning marital relations. In trying to minister to women with differing experiences and expectations, I have striven to stick close to the truth—the Word of God—but these answers are not dogmatic truth; they are thoughts by experts, colleagues and me. Each individual situation must be prayerfully considered and taken before the Lord. If you are really searching for personal answers, pray and seek the counsel of your church leadership.

Q: If my husband comes home drunk or high and wants sex, am I still to submit?

A: If it is your heart's desire to have sex with your husband, by all means do so. If, however, you are hesitant, it seems true intimacy cannot be achieved when one of the individuals is in an altered state of mind. God's desire for oneness (Gen. 2:24) requires that both people seek intimacy, not sex. I would suggest that you seek your husband's agreement to abstain while he is intoxicated and that you pray for restoration of your relationship with your husband—all so First Corinthians 7:5 is fulfilled: "Do not deprive one another except with consent for a time, that you may give yourselves to fasting and prayer; and come together again so that Satan does not tempt you because of your lack of self-control."

I think it would be wise to have a discussion with your husband when he is sober about how you feel regarding sex when he is high or drunk. Seek his agreement then, when he is in his right mind and can think clearly. In every single case, when you seek mutual consent to wait, you must do it with an attitude of respect—even if your husband is not acting in a respectful way (see 1 Cor. 7:3; 1 Pet. 3:1–7).

Q: If my husband is active in his addiction but is currently sober, must I have sex with him?

A: Let's take a step back. First, sin interferes with right relationship with God. Repentance is necessary before fellowship can be restored. Therefore, if your husband is pursuing a sinful lifestyle (repeating a sin he does not repent of), fellowship has been broken, and repentance is a necessary part of the restoration process. You may certainly choose to have sex with your husband in this situation. Although intercourse can be achieved when an offense lies between you, genuine intimacy cannot. And again, intimacy, not sex, is God's intended goal. If you agree not to have sex until repentance and reconciliation take place, use that time to pray (alone if necessary, together is ideal) and seek agreement. Strive to seek agreement before a problematic situation arises.

To investigate the importance of repentance and restoration read: Isa. 1:16; 59:2; Jer. 14:10–12; Ps. 66:18; 1 Cor. 7:4–5; 1 Pet. 3:7.

Q: What are my marital duties?

A: Submission (Eph. 5:22, 24; Col. 3:18; 1 Pet. 3:1); unconditional respect (Eph. 5:33); affection rendered to your husband (1 Cor. 7:3); mutual sexual intimacy (1 Cor. 7:4). If there are ongoing problems that are interfering with intimacy, professional help should be sought. If your husband's lifestyle/behavior/requests are contrary to the Word of God, posing harm to yourself or your children, remember that the church is an authority over your husband, and the Lord is a higher authority than the church (Heb. 13:7; 1 Cor. 11:3; Eph. 5:21–24).

Q: If we have had an argument which has not been resolved, do I have to agree to have sex?

A: A man's desire for physical intimacy may increase after conflict as a means to reconnect with his wife, but if there is a pattern of avoiding conflict resolution by "resolving" bad feelings through sexual intercourse, this should be addressed (but not in anger). Again, intimacy is achieved when there is emotional, spiritual and physical oneness. Talk through your conflict; this can develop emotional and spiritual intimacy and can increase the desire for physical intimacy. The Scripture clearly indicates that you should restore relationship quickly to avoid giving Satan a foothold in your marriage. (Read Matt. 5:22–24; 18:15; 21–22; 1 Cor. 7:5; Eph. 4:26–27.)

Q: If my husband has been with another woman, do I still have to be available to have sex? What if there is the possibility of sexually-transmitted disease?

A: No. I believe you biblically have two options. (But in either case, forgiveness is biblically commanded. See Eph. 4:32 and Matt. 18:35.)

i. *Forgiveness and restoration of the relationship.* "Now to the married I command, yet not I but the Lord: A wife is not to depart from her husband. But even if she does depart, let her remain unmarried or be reconciled to her husband" (1 Cor. 7:10–11).

ii. *Forgiveness and separation or divorce.* "And I say to you, whoever divorces his wife, *except for sexual immorality*, and marries another, commits adultery; and whoever marries her who is divorced commits adultery" (Matt. 19:9).

In the event that you determine between you and God that you will reconcile the marriage yet there is a possibility of disease, I recommend medical testing be done prior to the restoration of your sexual relationship. If it is determined that disease is present, you will at least be able to make an informed decision.

Q: If my husband is active in pornography, should I have sex when he wants it?

A: There are several ways to approach this question. The Bible clearly states that intimacy within a husband-wife relationship is the solution for sexual immorality if either person lacks self-control. "Nevertheless, because of sexual immorality, let each man have his own wife, and let each woman have her own husband. Let the husband render to his wife the affection due her, and likewise also the wife to her husband. The wife does not have authority over her own body, but the husband does. And likewise the husband does not have authority over his own body, but the wife does. Do not deprive one another except with consent for a time, that you may give yourselves to fasting and prayer; and come together again so that Satan does not tempt you because of your lack of self-control" (1 Cor. 7:2–5).

Therefore, if your husband approaches you acknowledging a temptation toward pornography before he acts on that temptation, I believe your willingness to respond to him is the very means God has set up "as the way of escape" for your husband so that he may "be able to bear it" successfully. (See 1 Cor. 10:13.)

One counselor shed this additional insight from Romans 12:21: "Do not be overcome by evil, but overcome evil with good." In other words, doing good to your husband may be the very thing God uses to help overcome evil in his life. It is not your place to judge your husband's heart. You may minister to your husband in this area, which may reduce the enticement of pornography. If you refuse to be intimate with him, it is entirely possible his pornography use will increase because he may see it as his only outlet. One wife sharing her personal experience in this area made the following statement: "I was always available because I loved my husband and wanted to be the one to satisfy him. Sometimes this prevented him from being unfaithful; sometimes it didn't."

A husband or wife actively involved in pornography wants to both be sexually immoral and have a sexual relationship with his/her spouse. Pornography involves seeking sexual pleasure outside the parameters of the marriage and therefore goes against the marriage vows. "You have heard that it was said to those of old, 'You shall not commit adultery.' But I say to you that whoever looks at a woman to lust for her has already committed adultery with her in his heart" (Matt. 5:27–28). As such, I believe repentance, forgiveness and reconciliation are necessary components to a vibrant, healthy, intimate relationship.

Q: Am I to be available to have sex with my husband on demand?

A: Sex is one of those topics that can be tough to talk about with spouses. It's much easier to discuss it with girlfriends. Why is that? It is possible that this situation (a demand for sex) arises because of a misunderstanding or lack of knowledge about each other. Do your best to foster openness in this area of relationship.

Of course, the wording "on demand" certainly raises questions about the quality of relationship between husband and wife. If a husband is demanding sex, it sounds like he misunderstands intimacy and is lacking love for his wife. However, if the wife repeatedly avoids intimacy or has withheld sex to make a statement or to punish her husband, I can understand why he may demand sex (right or wrong) out of sheer frustration. This situation sounds like one that could use some serious, open and honest discussion. If it is too difficult to do that, godly counsel should be sought.

One counselor provided these questions for contemplation: Is the husband truly inconsiderate, unreasonable, etc., or is the wife actually struggling with her own deeper issues? Is the wife interpreting her husband's behavior as demanding in light of these issues? Could it be a combination of both? The wife needs to ask herself if she feels her husband is demanding when he actually presenting an unwanted request. Is it a matter of preference—that he wants sex when she does not? If this is the case, there is nothing wrong with asking for a rain check that will be filled in short order, but it would be inappropriate to put him off indefinitely.

Q: What do I do if my husband wants sex and every cell of my body is screaming no?

A: First you need to ask yourself why every cell of your body is screaming no. Is there unresolved conflict? Seek to resolve it. "Moreover if your brother sins against you, go and tell him his fault between you and him alone. If he hears you, you have gained your brother" (Matt. 18:15).

Is there anger and bitterness? "And do not grieve the Holy Spirit of God, by whom you were sealed for the day of redemption. Let all bitterness, wrath, anger, clamor, and evil speaking be put away from you, with all malice. And be kind to one another, tenderhearted, forgiving one another, even as God in Christ forgave you" (Eph. 4:30–32).

Has resentment built up? There are deeper serious issues here that need to be addressed; godly counsel may be necessary.

Has there been a failure to connect emotionally? If your husband has failed to seek nonphysical intimacy, the intimacy of sex will be much more difficult. That said, I find no biblical support for two wrongs making a right. In other words, if your husband sins by failing to love you in the right way, you aren't granted amnesty. I don't believe his failure to love gives you freedom to say no. I know that might not sit well with some of you, but I don't think you'll find biblical evidence that says otherwise.

So when every cell is screaming no, here's what I would advise: Get alone for a few minutes (excuse yourself, and tell him you'll be right back). Cry out to God. Ask God for a tender servant's heart. Ask God to bless your obedience and for the strength to overcome your feelings. Lay everything before your Father. Ask God to impress upon your husband a like desire for emotional intimacy. Then wash your face and by faith believe that God will grant your request. Purpose to minister to your husband out of obedience to God. Believe it or not, ladies, we can act contrary to our emotions and be blessed because of it.

Q: What do I do if I'm repulsed by the thought of having sex?

A: Is the repulsion due to the act of sex or due to the idea of being intimate with your husband?

God designed sex for the mutual enjoyment of the husband and the wife. "Therefore a man shall leave his father and mother and be joined to his wife, and they shall become one flesh" (Gen. 2:24). Sexual intimacy is an expression of spiritual, emotional and physical oneness. Therefore, repulsion to sex is the opposite of what God desires for us.

i. Could the repulsion be due to childhood abuses? Seek godly counsel.

ii. Could the repulsion be a result of disobeying Ephesians 4:26–27? "'Be angry and do not sin'; do not let the sun go down on your wrath, nor give place to the devil."

iii. Could the repulsion be physical/hygienic (failure to shower, shave, etc.)? Lovingly and respectfully share your concerns. (Do not use words like "repulsed.") Give your husband a vision of how things might be different if he attended to these matters.

Q: What if my husband wants me to do something sexually that I'm uncomfortable with; should I do it?

A: Sexual intimacy is a mutual relationship. In that regard you are free to enjoy all the pleasures sex has to offer. I would suggest that when a request is made, you prayerfully consider it rather than giving a flat out no. If after consideration you are still not comfortable, I believe it is fine to decline and to seek other means of mutual satisfaction. Fellow counselors suggest discussing it and seeking agreement on what *is* permissible. These discussions are best handled prior to sex.

Q: What do I do if my husband wants sex much more than I do?

A: This is not particularly uncommon. I would suggest discussing the situation so there is mutual understanding. Ladies, this may be an area where you will need to die to self and put your husband's desires above your own. "Then Jesus said to His disciples, 'If anyone desires to come after Me, let him deny himself, and take up his cross, and follow Me'" (Matt. 16:24).

i. Do your best to be well-rested and undistracted. Make opportunities for the two of you to be alone. Ask the Lord for balance and wisdom (see James 1:5).

ii. Be thankful. Scripture tells us to be thankful in all things. It would be easy to focus on the "burden" of frequent sex, but if you were to step back and consider what you have to be thankful for, it may change your entire attitude. Be thankful he's coming to you. Be thankful he enjoys being intimate with you. Be thankful for all the ways he is a good husband. Be thankful he finds you attractive and enticing. Be thankful that sexual intimacy is a gift from God. One counselor suggested looking for ways to increase your desire. Buy some sexy lingerie (and then actually wear it), light candles, run a hot tub, give each other body massages—you get the idea. Plan to enjoy the encounter; the anticipation can increase your desire for intimacy.

Q: What do I do if I want sex much more than my husband?

A: i. Is there a physical problem? Suggest he see a doctor.

ii. Do you regularly fail to climax? Perhaps he's too embarrassed or feels inadequate to meet your needs; this can be a real hit on a man's view of himself. Get a good book on sexual technique and read it together. (See our suggested book list at the end of the chapter.)

iii. Be creative. Find ways to entice him.

If these problems continue, seek godly counsel.

Q: What if my husband shows no interest in intimacy?

A: An open, honest, frank discussion is necessary.

i. Is there pornography involvement? If yes, seek counsel.

ii. Is there any evidence of sexual sin? If yes, seek counsel.

Be bold. If you are sitting back waiting for him to initiate all the time, you may sit a long time alone. Initiate intimacy. Be creative; find ways to entice him. Get rid of the TV in the bedroom or whatever else draws your attention away from each other. If this problem persists, seek godly counsel.

Q: My husband shows me no affection—what do I do?

A: Your husband's failure to fulfill his part of First Corinthians 7:3 does not negate your obedience to your part. "Let the husband render to his wife the affection due her, and likewise also the wife to her husband."

Perhaps your husband is uncomfortable with public displays of affection, so start at home. Be affectionate toward your husband, even if he doesn't respond. Talk to him about how you feel. If the problem continues, seek godly counsel.

Q: What if I have been sexually abused and am fearful of sex?

A: If there is physical pain associated with intimacy, see your doctor to make sure everything is in proper order. Be open with your husband. This might require baby steps to overcome your fear. One expert said to be fearful but keep moving forward. I would suggest you focus on your love for your husband and your desire to please him, rather than on the sex act itself. By all means, seek godly counsel to resolve these issues.

In Conclusion

As I said earlier, this has been the most difficult chapter I have written in this curriculum. My prayer is that I have rightly handled God's Word. That said, you may not agree with my conclusions; if you can find biblical support for your opinion, then by all means disagree. If not, please take these lessons to heart and pray!

Before I close this chapter, I want to bring us back to a few certainties that are applicable in a marital relationship. After all is said and done, "And now abide faith, hope, love, these three; but the greatest of these is love" (1 Cor.13:13). Each of these three elements is vital to a biblical, God-honoring, fulfilling, intimate marriage:

Faith

Considering the biblical accounts of great men and women of faith, I have come to the conclusion that everything we do of eternal value requires faith. Look at Noah; he built an ark for a flood when he had never seen rain (see Gen. 6–8). Then there was Abraham whom God called to sacrifice his son, his only son, whom he loved; Abraham knew Isaac was the son of promise, and it didn't make much sense to kill his only heir, but he obeyed anyway (see Gen. 22). How about Moses? He kept obeying God, even as time after time Pharaoh refused his request (see Exod. 3–12). Gideon took an army of three hundred men up against a people "as numerous as locusts" (see Judg. 7:12). The Bible is replete with illustrations of faith.

Just what is faith? According to Hebrews 11:1, faith is believing beyond what we know, taste, touch, smell, hear or see: "Faith is the substance of things hoped for, the evidence of things not seen."

How is faith required in the area of intimacy? I believe it requires faith to act upon what you know to be true from the Bible, even when it doesn't feel true. A woman who steps out in faith to minister to her husband sexually—even when she doesn't have warm fuzzies for him—requires the power of the Holy Spirit living through her to make her action pleasing to God. "But without faith it is impossible to please Him, for he who comes to God must believe that He is, and that He is a rewarder of those who diligently seek Him" (Heb. 11:6).

Do you want the sexual intimacy in your marriage to be God-honoring, God-glorifying and God-pleasing? Live it out by faith.

Our Christian walk and growth is a process of dying to ourselves and allowing Christ to live through us. "I have been crucified with Christ; it is no longer I who live, but Christ lives in me; and the life which I now live in the flesh I live by faith in the Son of God, who loved me and gave Himself for me" (Gal. 2:20).

Hope

Do you find yourself believing there is no hope for the intimate aspect of your marriage? Do not despair. When you allow yourself to despair, Satan has you right where he wants you. Do not let him win this battle. As a child of God, the Holy Spirit dwells within you, and therefore there is hope. "Or do you not know that your body is the temple of the Holy Spirit who is in you, whom you have from God, and you are not your own? For you were bought at a price; therefore glorify God in your body and in your spirit, which are God's" (1 Cor. 6:19–20).

"Now may the God of hope fill you with all joy and peace in believing, that you may abound in hope by the power of the Holy Spirit" (Rom. 15:13).

Love

"But the greatest of these is love" (1 Cor. 13:13).

You know, maybe the bottom line in all this is, as believers, we are called to love our brother. What

does love look like? Please read First Corinthians 13, starting in verse 4, and record the characteristics of love that you find. _____
_____
_____

"A new commandment I give to you, that you love one another; as I have loved you, that you also love one another" (John 13:34).

How has God loved you? _____
_____
_____

"Therefore, as the elect of God, holy and beloved, put on tender mercies, kindness, humility, meekness, longsuffering; bearing with one another, and forgiving one another, if anyone has a complaint against another; even as Christ forgave you, so you also must do" (Col. 3:12–13).

"Let all that you do be done with love" (1 Cor. 16:14).

"And above all things have fervent love for one another, for 'love will cover a multitude of sins.' Be hospitable to one another without grumbling" (1 Pet. 4:8–9).

What sins might your love enable you to overlook? _____
_____

"By this we know love, because He laid down His life for us. And we also ought to lay down our lives for the brethren. But whoever has this world's good, and sees his brother in need, and shuts up his heart from him, how does the love of God abide in him?" (1 John 3:16–17).

How is God prompting you to lay down your life? _____
_____
_____

As you work to apply the practical lessons learned in this chapter, remember that God is with you every step of the way.

God is at work. "Now may the God of peace Himself sanctify you completely; and may your whole spirit, soul, and body be preserved blameless at the coming of our Lord Jesus Christ. He who calls you is faithful, who also will do it" (1 Thess. 5:23–24).

God is conforming you to the image of Jesus Christ. "And we, who with unveiled faces all reflect the Lord's glory, are being transformed into his likeness with ever-increasing glory, which comes from the Lord, who is the Spirit" (2 Cor. 3:18, NIV). "For whom He foreknew, He also predestined to be conformed to the image of His Son, that He might be the firstborn among many brethren" (Rom. 8:29).

God empowers and makes provision for you. "And my God shall supply all your need according to His riches in glory by Christ Jesus" (Phil. 4:19).

"As His divine power has given to us all things that pertain to life and godliness, through the knowledge of Him who called us by glory and virtue, by which have been given to us exceedingly great and precious promises, that through these you may be partakers of the divine nature, having escaped the corruption that is in the world through lust" (2 Pet. 1:3–4).

Intimacy is a very personal issue, and God has a lot to say about it. He created our bodies to find pleasure with our spouses within the context of marriage. It is for our enjoyment and delight. God delights to give us good things, and as we step out in faith and obey His commandments, we will be positively transformed and He will be glorified.

Additional Resources

Every Man's Battle by Stephen Arterburn and Fred Stoeker

Every Woman's Battle by Shannon Etheridge

Sacred Sex by Tim Allan Gardner

The Intimacy Cover-up by P. Roger Hillerstrom and Karlyn Hillerstrom

Real Questions, Real Answers About Sex by Dr. Louis and Melissa McBurney

False Intimacy by Dr. Harry W. Schaumburg

Intended for Pleasure by Dr. Ed Wheat

Application Questions

1. What one or two statements impacted me from this chapter?

   a. _____

   b. _____

2. How can I apply it/them to my life today and begin to pursue positive growth? _____
   _____

3. What one step am I willing to take to move toward heart change in my reactions, behavior or attitude? _____
   _____

4. What do I learn about God from this chapter? _____
   _____

5. How does His Word (the Bible) confirm this? _____
   _____
   _____

And the Journey Continues . . .

by Diane Hunt

You shall write on them all the words of this law, when you have crossed over, that you may enter the land which the LORD *your God is giving you, 'a land flowing with milk and honey,' just as the* LORD *God of your fathers promised you.*

Deuteronomy 27:3

14

One comment we've received on this study in overwhelming numbers is that it forces women to take their eyes off their husbands and start looking at themselves and their own walks with Christ. I trust your heart has been challenged as you too have considered your personal journey with God. You've likely wrestled with accepting God's hand in your suffering, with how similar you are to the addicted person in your life, with how anger, bitterness, worry and fear have robbed you of peace and contentment and with how to submit to and respect your husband in obedience to Christ. It probably has not been an easy journey, but I trust you have been blessed. I pray you've learned how to live out Christ in your life even when your mate is not, how to forgive him biblically and how to embrace the deep, rich intimate relationship Jesus Christ longs to have with you.

When things seem to be in constant change and instability abounds, remember that God's Word is forever settled in heaven (Ps. 119:89) and that He "is the same yesterday, today, and forever" (Heb. 13:8).

One of God's goals in your life is to conform you to the image of His Son, which means all that you are going through has purpose and meaning; you are being transformed. "But we all, with unveiled face, beholding as in a mirror the glory of the Lord, are being transformed into the same image from glory to glory, just as by the Spirit of the Lord" (2 Cor. 3:18). He is conforming you to the image of Jesus Christ. "For whom He foreknew, He also predestined to be conformed to the image of His Son, that He might be the firstborn among many brethren" (Rom. 8:29). God will finish what He has begun in you. "Being confident of this very thing, that He who has begun a good work in you will complete it until the day of Jesus Christ" (Phil. 1:6).

God is at work in your life in the midst of your circumstances. "Now may the God of peace Himself sanctify you completely; and may your whole spirit, soul, and body be preserved blameless at the coming of our Lord Jesus Christ. He who calls you is faithful, who also will do it" (1 Thess. 5:23–24).

The process of growth in the life of every believer is progressive; we are not perfected at the moment of salvation. We are declared righteous (known as justification), but we are progressively made more and more like Jesus (known as sanctification) until we see Him face to face. There will be many times when knowing that you are in the process of growth and change will bring comfort to your heart. God is up to something amazing in your life, and He is using your circumstances and the people in your life to accomplish it.

Sister, do not grow weary. Satan would delight to wear you down so you'll give up. When you are weary, press in closer to your Groom, your Savior, your Friend; trust God to strengthen you. "And let us not grow weary while doing good, for in due season we shall reap if we do not lose heart" (Gal. 6:9).

And the Journey Continues . . .

Persevere and press on, one step at a time. "Even the youths shall faint and be weary, And the young men shall utterly fall, But those who wait on the Lord Shall renew their strength; They shall mount up with wings like eagles, They shall run and not be weary, They shall walk and not faint" (Isa. 40:30–31).

For years the verse that appeared on every letter sent from our office was Romans 15:13: "Now may the God of hope fill you with all joy and peace in believing, that you may abound in hope by the power of the Holy Spirit." Often when women come to us, they are hanging on by a thread, weary and hopeless. One of our goals in this study is to renew your hope and to give you a hope that will not be dashed by undesirable circumstances or shattered by poor choices—a hope that is solidly grounded in God. When you place your trust in God rather than in your spouse or yourself, you will find Him faithful. You can trust Him to keep His word. Stand by faith on the word of God; you will *always find it true*.

Remember that God is sovereign. He is King of the universe and is in control of every aspect, every situation in life and every single molecule in the universe. Nothing, absolutely nothing, is outside His awareness, power and touch. He is God, and there is no other.

God is Redeemer. He redeems that which is meant for evil and turns it to good (Gen. 50:20). Why does that offer hope to you today? As you look around and see wicked, evil, painful things in the world, know beyond all doubt that God will redeem it all. In the end He will orchestrate life for your best good and His greatest glory (Rom. 8:28).

I trust as you have journeyed through this book and have seen the raging waters of the Jordan River in your own life, you have also heard in your heart the voice of God, calling you to step out in faith and to trust Him to lead you across to a place of promise and rest.

I pray your encounter with God and His Word has been a blessing to your heart and spirit. Even after you put this book aside, carry with you the truths God has given you. Treasure your sweeter, deeper relationship with Jesus Christ. As we part, He goes with you.

Appendix: My True Identity[1]

The following is a list of truths concerning who you are in Christ. These are what God says about you; they reveal your true identity. You might like to mark these in your Bible along with other "identity" verses you will find on your own.

John 1:12	I am a child of God. (Rom. 8:16)
John 15:1, 5	I am a branch on the Vine—Christ, a channel of His life to bear the fruit He produces.
John 15:15	I am Christ's friend.
John 15:16	I am chosen and appointed by Christ.
John 16:27	I am loved by my Father.
Acts 1:8	I am a personal witness of Christ for Christ.
Romans 3:24	I have been redeemed.
Romans 5:1	I have been justified and am at peace with God.
Romans 6:1–6	I died in Christ to the power of sin's rule over me.
Romans 6:7	I have been freed from sin's power over me.
Romans 6:18	I am a slave of righteousness.
Romans 6:22	I am enslaved to God.
Romans 8:1	I am forever free from condemnation.
Romans 8:14	I am a son (daughter) of God. God is literally my "Papa" or "Dad." (Gal. 3:26; 4:6; Rom. 8:15)
Romans 8:17	I am an heir of God and a fellow heir with Christ.
Romans 11:16	I am holy.
Romans 15:7	Christ accepts me.
First Corinthians 1:2	I have been sanctified.
First Corinthians 1:30	I have been placed in Christ by God's doing. Christ is now my wisdom from God, my righteousness, my sanctification and my redemption.
First Corinthians 2.12	I have received the Spirit of God that I might know the things freely given to me by God.

First Corinthians 2:16	I have the mind of Christ.
First Corinthians 3:16	I am the temple (home) of God; His Spirit (His life) dwells in me (1 Cor. 6:19).
First Corinthians 6:17	I am joined to the Lord, and I am one Spirit with Him.
First Corinthians 6:19–20	I have been bought with a price; I am not my own; I belong to God.
First Corinthians 12:27	I am a member of Christ's body (Eph. 5:30).
Second Corinthians 1:21	I have been established in Christ and anointed by God.
Second Corinthians 2:14	He always leads me in His triumph in Christ.
Second Corinthians 3:17	I have liberty because of Christ.
Second Corinthians 5:14–15	I no longer live for myself but for Christ.
Second Corinthians 5:17	I am a new creation.
Second Corinthians 5:18–19	I am reconciled to God and am a minister of reconciliation.
Second Corinthians 5:21	I am the righteousness of God in Christ.
Galatians 2:20	I was crucified with Christ, and it is no longer [the old] I who live, but Christ lives in [the new] me; the life I now live is Christ's life.
Galatians 4:6–7	I am a child of God and an heir.
Ephesians 1:1	I am a saint. (1 Cor. 1:2; Phil. 1:1; Col. 1:2)
Ephesians 1:3	I am blessed with every spiritual blessing.
Ephesians 1:4	I was chosen in Christ before the foundation of the world to be holy and without blame before Him.
Ephesians 1:5	I am adopted as God's child through Jesus Christ.
Ephesians 1:6	I am accepted in the Beloved.
Ephesians 1:7–8	I have been redeemed, forgiven, and am a recipient of His lavish grace.
Ephesians 2:5	I have been made alive together with Christ.
Ephesians 2:6	I have been raised up and seated with Christ in heaven.
Ephesians 2:10	I am God's workmanship, created in Christ to do the things He prepared beforehand that I should do.
Ephesians 2:13	I have been brought near to God.
Ephesians 2:18	I have direct access to God through the Holy Spirit.
Ephesians 2:19	I am a fellow citizen with the saints and a member of God's household.
Ephesians 3:6	I am a fellow heir, a member of Christ's body and a fellow partaker of God's promise in Christ Jesus.
Ephesians 3:12	I may approach God with boldness and confidence.

Ephesians 4:24	I am righteous and holy.
Philippians 3:20	I am a citizen of heaven.
Philippians 4:7	His peace guards my heart and mind.
Philippians 4:19	God will supply all my needs: physical, psychological and spiritual.
Colossians 1:13	I have been delivered from the domain of darkness and transferred to the kingdom of Christ.
Colossians 1:14	I have been redeemed and forgiven of all my sins; the debt against me has been cancelled. (Col.2:13-14)
Colossians 1:27	I have the Spirit of Christ Himself in me.
Colossians 2:7	I have been firmly rooted in Christ and am now being built up and established in Him.
Colossians 2:10	I have been made complete in Christ.
Colossians 2:11	I have been spiritually circumcised; my old, unregenerate nature has been removed.
Colossians 2:12-13	I have been buried, raised and made alive with Christ in God.
Colossians 3:1	I have been raised up with Christ.
Colossians 3:3	The old "I" has died, and my present life is now hidden with Christ in God.
Colossians 3:4	Christ is now my life.
Colossians 3:12	I am chosen by God, holy and dearly loved. (Acts 10:15)
First Thessalonians 5:5	I am a child of light, not of darkness.
Second Timothy 1:7	I have been given a spirit of power, love and a sound mind.
Second Timothy 1:9	I have been saved and called [set apart] according to His purpose and grace.
Hebrews 2:11	Because I am sanctified and am one with Christ, God is not ashamed to call me His child.
Hebrews 3:1	I am a holy partaker of a heavenly calling.
Hebrews 3:14	I am a partaker of Christ.
Hebrews 4:16	I may come boldly before the throne and receive mercy and find grace to help me in the time of need.
Hebrews 10:10	I have been sanctified by His will. (Acts 10:15)
First Peter 2:5	I am one of God's living stones, and I am being built up (along with other saints) as a spiritual house.
First Peter 2:9–10	I am part of a chosen race, a royal priesthood, a holy nation, a people of God's own possession.

First Peter 2:11	I am an alien and a stranger to this world where I live temporarily.
Second Peter 1:4	I have been given His precious and magnificent promises by which I am a partaker of God's divine nature.
Isaiah 61:10	I wear robes of righteousness.
Isaiah 49:16	My name is written in the palm of His hand.

Endnotes

Foreword

1. Rev. William Raws, "What's the Difference: The Message of the Victorious Christian Life," accessed June 1, 2011, http://www.americaskeswick.org/files/Documents/Brochures/Difference.pdf.

Chapter 2

1. James Strong, *Strong's Exhaustive Concordance of the Bible* (Grand Rapids: Zondervan, 1980).

Chapter 3

1. Paul David Tripp, *Instruments of Change: How God Can Use You to Help People Grow* (Glenside, PA: Christian Counseling & Educational Foundation, 2000).

2. Bill Bright, "Have You Heard of the Four Spiritual Laws?" (Orlando, FL: New Life Publications, 1965).

Chapter 4

1. *The American Heritage®Stedman's Medical Dictionary* (Boston: Houghton Mifflin, 2002).

2. Edward Welch, *Addictions: A Banquet in the Grave* (Phillipsburg, NJ: P&R Publishing, 2001).

3. Ibid.

4. M.G. Easton, *Easton's Bible Dictionary* (Oxford: Benediction Classics, 1894).

5. *Merriam-Webster Online Dictionary*. Merriam-Webster, Inc., s.v. "idolatry," accessed February 12, 2011, http://merriam-webster.com/dictionary.

6. Welch, *Addictions: A Banquet in the Grave.*

7. Beth Moore, *Breaking Free: Making Liberty in Christ a Reality in Life* (Nashville: Lifeway, 1999), VHS series.

8. Ibid.

9. Tim Jackson and Jeff Olson, "When We Just Can't Stop" (RBC Ministries, 1996), accessed June 21, 2011, http://web001.rbc.org/pdf/discovery-series/when-we-just-cant-stop-overcoming-addiction.pdf.

10. Ibid.

11. Ibid.

12. Welch, *Addictions: A Banquet in the Grave*.

13. Ibid.

Chapter 5

1. Paraphrased from Joni Eareckson Tada and Steve Estes, *When God Weeps* (Grand Rapids: Zondervan, 1997).

2. This excerpt is copied from the Biblical Counseling Foundation's 480-page in-depth discipleship manual entitled *Self-Confrontation* (1991 edition) by permission of the Biblical Counseling Foundation.

3. P.B. Wilson, *Liberated through Submission: God's Design for Freedom in All Relationships* (Eugene, OR: Harvest House, 1997).

4. Ibid.

5. Ibid.

6. *The American Heritage® Dictionary of the English Language*, Fourth Edition, s.v. "repent," accessed June 22, 2011, http://www.thefreedictionary.com/repent.

7. Jack Hayford, *The Spirit-Filled Life Bible: A Personal Study Bible Unveiling All God's Fullness in All God's Word* (Nashville: Thomas Nelson, 1991).

Chapter 6

1. Beth Moore, *Believing God* (Nashville: B&H Publishing, 2002).

2. *Merriam-Webster Online Dictionary*. Merriam-Webster, Inc., s.v. "sarcasm," accessed February 12, 2011, www.merriam-webster.com/dictionary/sarcasm.

3. *Merriam-Webster Online Dictionary*. Merriam-Webster, Inc., s.v. "nagging," accessed February 12, 2011, www.merriam-webster.com/dictionary/nagging.

4. *Merriam-Webster Online Dictionary*. Merriam-Webster, Inc., s.v. "critical," accessed February 12, 2011, www.merriam-webster.com/dictionary/critical.

5. *Merriam-Webster Online Dictionary*. Merriam-Webster, Inc., s.v. "encourage," accessed February 12, 2011, www.merriam-webster.com/dictionary/encourage.

6. *Merriam-Webster Online Dictionary*. Merriam-Webster, Inc., s.v. "edify," accessed February 12, 2011, www.merriam-webster.com/dictionary/edify.

7. *Merriam-Webster Online Dictionary*. Merriam-Webster, Inc., s.v. "bless," accessed February 12, 2011, www.merriam-webster.com/dictionary/bless.

8. *Merriam-Webster Online Dictionary*. Merriam-Webster, Inc., s.v. "instruct," accessed February 12, 2011, www.merriam-webster.com/dictionary/instruct.

9. *Merriam-Webster Online Dictionary*. Merriam-Webster, Inc., s.v. "exhort," accessed February 12, 2011, www.merriam-webster.com/dictionary/exhort.

10. *Merriam-Webster Online Dictionary*. Merriam-Webster, Inc., s.v. "admonish," accessed February 12, 2011, www.merriam-webster.com/dictionary/admonish.

11. *Merriam-Webster Online Dictionary*. Merriam-Webster, Inc., s.v. "reprimand," accessed February 12, 2011, www.merriam-webster.com/dictionary/reprimand.

12. *Merriam-Webster Online Dictionary*. Merriam-Webster, Inc., s.v. "comfort," accessed February 12, 2011, www.merriam-webster.com/dictionary/comfort.

Chapter 7

1. Personal notes from Dr. Dan Skogen's seminar on anger in semester three of a CJBI Biblical Counseling training course.

2. Billy Graham, *The A to Z Guide to Bible Application,* developed by The Livingstone Corporation (Carol Stream, IL: Tyndale, 1996).

3. Shannon B. Rainey, "Why Am I So Angry?" *Discipleship Journal,* (May/June 1995).

4. Jay E. Adams, *What Do You Do When Anger Gets the Upper Hand?* (Phillipsburg, NJ: P&R Publishing, 1975).

5. Rainey, "Why Am I So Angry?"

6. Adams, *What Do You Do When Anger Gets the Upper Hand?*

7. Ibid.

8. Ibid.

9. Stuart Briscoe, *Secrets of the Heart: Lessons from the Psalms* (Colorado Springs, CO: Harold Shaw Publishers, 1999).

10. Beth Moore, *Praying God's Word* (Nashville: B&H Publishing, 2000).

11. Briscoe, *Secrets of the Heart*.

12. Elyse Fitzpatrick and Carol Cornish, *Women Helping Women* (Eugene, OR: Harvest House, 1997).

13. Gary Chapman, *The Other Side of Love: Handling Anger in a Godly Way* (Chicago: Moody Press, 1999).

14. Fitzpatrick and Cornish, *Women Helping Women*.

Chapter 8

1. Everett L. Worthington, "Forgiveness," in *The Bible for Hope: Caring for People God's Way*, ed. Tim Clinton (Nashville: Thomas Nelson, 2001).

2. *Merriam-Webster Online Dictionary*. Merriam-Webster, Inc., s.v. "forgiveness," accessed February 12, 2011, www.merriam-webster.com/dictionary/forgiveness.

3. Grace Ketterman and David Hazard, *When You Can't Say "I Forgive You"* (Colorado Springs, CO: NavPress, 2000).

4. Stephen Arterburn and Dr. David Stoop, *The Power of Forgiveness* (Laguna Beach, CA: New Life Ministries, 2005), CD.

5. Rob Tarnovski and Nancy Cole-Shallow, *War of Words: The Need for Forgiveness* (Philadelphia: Bethel Fellowship, 2006), CD.

6. Robert D. Jones, *Forgiveness: I Just Can't Forgive Myself* (Phillipsburg, NJ: P&R Publishing, 2000).

7. Kay Arthur, *Lord, Heal My Hurts* (Colorado Springs, CO: Waterbrook Press, 1989).

8. Rob Tarnovski and Nancy Cole-Shallow, *War of Words*.

9. *Merriam-Webster Online Dictionary*, Merriam-Webster, Inc., s.v. "apology," accessed February 12, 2011, www.merriam-webster/dictionary/apology.

Chapter 9

1. This excerpt is copied from the Biblical Counseling Foundation's 480-page in-depth discipleship manual entitled *Self-Confrontation* (1991 edition) by permission of the Biblical Counseling Foundation.

2. Neil Anderson and Mike and Julia Quarles, *One Day at a Time: The Devotional for Overcomers* (Ventura, CA: Regal Books, 2000).